FAITH CLINIC

VOLUME XXVI

HOPELESSNESS EDITION

*I Came for Healing, But All I Got Was
Conviction And A Scripture*

DR. PATRICIA S. TANNER

IBG Publications, Inc.

Published by I.B.G. Publications, Inc., a Power to Wealth Company

Web address: www.ibgpublications.com

admin@ibgpublications.com / 904-419-9810

Copyright, 2025 by Patricia S. Tanner

IBG Publications, Inc., Jacksonville, FL

ISBN: 978-1-971850-13-9

Tanner, Patricia S.

Faith Clinic, Volume XXVI-Hopelessness Edition- *I Came for Healing, But All I Got Was Conviction and a Scripture*

Printed in the United States of America.

DEDICATION

To the ones who are tired of trying… and even more tired of pretending. To those who showed up for healing but found themselves confronted instead. To every heart that has whispered, "I don't know if I can do this anymore," but kept going anyway.

This book is dedicated to you.

To the ones sitting in silent battles, wrestling with faith, and learning that even in hopeless moments, God is still working beneath the surface.

May you find strength in the breaking, clarity in the conviction, and hope in the process you didn't choose.

You are not as far gone as you feel. And you are not beyond healing.

With compassion and truth,

DR. PATRICIA S. TANNER

The Faith Doctor

TABLE OF CONTENTS

INTRODUCTION

You thought it was a spa day for your soul, turns out it's surgery with no anesthesia. Welcome to growth.

You didn't come here expecting a confrontation. You came for a vibe. Maybe a hot tea, a blanket, a gentle word from the Lord about your future spouse, and a Pinterest-ready quote like "You are enough." You wanted healing, peace, answers, and possibly some spiritual exfoliation, a light scrub for your trauma, not deep heart surgery.

But instead, you walked in and got wrecked. Not by a therapist. Not by your pastor. But by one random verse that sucker-punched your pride so hard you nearly uninstalled your Bible app. You asked for comfort, and God handed you conviction. You wanted a break, and He gave you a breakdown, the kind that exposes what's broken. No filter. No sugar. Just raw, holy disruption.

Let's be honest, healing doesn't feel like healing at first. It feels like being exposed. Like the Holy Spirit shining a flashlight into the storage closet of your heart and saying, "Uh... what's this mess?" And you're standing there like, "Wait, I thought this was going to be about peace and purpose. Not... whatever this is." Oh, but this *is* the process. Because God doesn't do surface-level healing. He digs. He cuts. He calls out the infection and won't let you leave until the root's out.

This isn't a spa. It's an operating room. And you don't get to leave with your edges laid and your soul untouched. Here's what nobody tells you in church announcements: **conviction is a gift**. Not a punishment. Not spiritual shame. Not the end of the story. But the beginning of real change. And sometimes, all it takes is one verse, one unexpected moment, to wreck your excuses and force you to admit, "I'm not okay. But maybe that's the point."

This book is not about pretending. It's about processing. It's about the version of healing that doesn't trend well online because it's too gritty, too painful, too honest. It's about the kind of growth that comes after God ruins your comfort zone and rewrites your coping strategies.

So, buckle up. Take off your spiritual makeup. Leave your curated testimony at the door. Because what's about to happen here isn't pretty, but it *will* be worth it. This is the Faith Clinic. And the Doctor? He's not handing out lollipops; He's wielding a scalpel. You walked into this thing thinking it was going to be cute. Maybe a journal session with soft worship music in the background, a pumpkin spice latte, and a little devotional about God's love, preferably the "nothing is required of you" kind. You didn't expect to be diagnosed. You didn't expect the Holy Spirit to pull up receipts from five years ago. You just wanted healing. But instead, you got hit with truth. The kind that doesn't pat you on the back, it yanks you out of bed and says, "We need to talk."

And now here you are, sitting in a soul clinic you didn't know you signed up for, wrapped in a thin hospital gown of conviction, holding a clipboard with questions like: *When was the last time you forgave someone who didn't apologize? Are you praying or just venting on TikTok? Have you confused numbness for peace?* The truth? You didn't come here for a whole intervention. You came for vibes. But God has this way of ignoring what we want and going after what we need.

Healing sounds lovely until you realize it starts with confrontation. Not with other people, with yourself. That's the twist no one warns you about. To be truly healed, you must admit you're sick. And not in a trendy, "we all have issues" kind of way. No, you must confront the quiet parts of your soul that you've kept on Do Not Disturb. That resentment you've dressed up as boundaries. That fear you labeled as discernment. That pride that's been rebranded as "self-awareness." The clinic exposes all of it. And it doesn't give you a blanket and peppermint tea. It hands you a scalpel and says, "Let's cut this out before it kills you."

If you're still reading, it means some part of you, no matter how tiny, is ready. Ready for the real kind of healing. Not the Instagram-filtered, coffee-shop Christianity that gives you a temporary high. No, you're ready for the kind of healing that keeps you up at night because you're finally being honest. The kind that breaks you down before it builds you back up. The kind that doesn't just comfort you but *calls you higher.*

Let's get something straight: this book is not here to fix you. You're not a broken appliance. You're a human being made in the image of a holy, healing God who refuses to let you stay spiritually shallow. This is not self-help. This is surrender. And no, it's not comfortable. But it is divine. Because the truth is, many of us don't need another feeling good moment. We need a wake-up call. We don't need another verse stitched on a hoodie; we need it stitched into our hearts.

So, if you're tired of fake healing that doesn't last... If you're exhausted from pretending, you're okay when you're drowning... If you're done running from the one place that could help... Then welcome. You're in the right place. The Faith Clinic isn't pretty. But it's holy. It isn't easy. But it's necessary. It isn't fast. But it's faithful. Here, conviction is the sign that your heart still works. Here, truth hurts, but it heals deeper than anything comfort ever could. Here, you don't get discharged until denial dies and deliveries are born.

So, take a deep breath. You're not being punished. You're being transformed. You didn't come for conviction, but it found you anyway. Now lean in. This isn't the healing you asked for. It is the healing you were created for.

The Spa Day That Turned Into Surgery

You ever walk into something expecting a vibe, only to leave with a revelation that wrecks your whole week? That's what this book is. You thought you were signing up for a peaceful retreat with ambient worship music and cucumber water, but surprise, God brought the scalpel, the lights are on, and there's nowhere to hide. Welcome to the Faith Clinic, where "healing" isn't a playlist, it's an encounter. And sometimes, healing doesn't start until something painful gets touched.

We've glamorized growth. We've filtered transformation until it fits neatly into Instagram captions and Sunday morning sound bites. But the real stuff? The soul work? That's ugly. That's messy. That's spiritual surgery with no anesthesia. It's God pressing on bruises you thought were healed. It's the Holy Spirit pulling receipts on patterns you thought were "just part of your personality." It's scripture that doesn't comfort you; it confronts you. And conviction that doesn't pat your back, it rips the mask off your face.

This isn't one of those books that tells you to just "pray it away" or "have more faith." If that worked, we wouldn't be here. You're not reading this because you're weak, you're reading it because you're ready. Ready to be more emotionally managed. Ready to be spiritually mature. Ready to stop dressing your wounds with worship songs while bleeding out in your bedroom. You're here because, somewhere deep inside, you know that growth doesn't happen in padded pews, it happens in spiritual surgery. And if you're going to let God do the cutting, you might as well know what's on the table.

Let's be clear: this isn't about fixing you. This is about forming you. There's a difference. Fixing implies you're broken and need to be put back together like a dropped iPhone. But formation? That's divine. That's what God did with dust and breath in Genesis. He didn't patch Adam together, He formed him. Intentionally. Carefully. Slowly. And that's what this clinic is all about. Not putting a bandage over a bullet wound but forming you from the inside out.

We live in a culture that's obsessed with relief. Numb the pain. Escape the pressure. Curate your peace. But relief is not the same as healing. Healing requires honesty. It demands confrontation. It insists that you feel what you've been avoiding, sit with what you've been escaping, and talk to the God you've been ghosting. And sometimes, that starts with a rude awakening: you didn't come to the clinic for a nap. You came for surgery. That means something's about to change.

This book isn't soft. It's sacred. It's not cozy. It's confrontational. It's for the ones who are done playing healed and ready to walk out whole. It's for the girl who prays with tears in her eyes but still feels like fraud. It's for the guy who knows the Bible backwards but can't feel God in the silence. It's for the leaders, the wounded, the tired, the over-churched and under-pastored, the ones who almost walked away but stayed one more day just in case God showed up. This is for you.

We're not playing church in these pages. We're unlearning survival and relearning surrender. We're trading quick fixes for deep formation. We're exchanging religion for relationships. We admit that conviction is a form of care and that discomfort is a doorway to deliverance. And we're doing all of this, not because it's trendy, but because healing was never meant to be cute. It was meant to be Christ-centered.

So yeah, you came for healing. But what if healing starts with heartbreak? What if it begins when the Holy Spirit hands you a mirror instead of a microphone? What if scripture doesn't fix your situation but exposes your soul? And what if, at the end of it all, you don't walk away with a spa-like peace, but a scar that proves you survived the surgery?

We live in a world that sells ease as a virtue. Everything must be convenient, instantaneous, and painless. You want food? There's an app. You want fame? Go viral. You want answers? Google them. But growth? Real, deep, lasting transformation? That one doesn't come with a shortcut. And yet, that's what most of us expect when we walk into the presence of God. We assume that showing up in a church building will do what years of trauma, cycles of bad choices, and buried pain haven't been able to fix. We think we're going to get a warm towel and soft music. Instead, God hands us a scalpel and whispers, "Let's deal with this."

Spiritual growth doesn't happen in comfort. It happens in confrontation. And not the loud, dramatic kind that plays out in front of people, but the quiet, soul-shaking moments where God sits you down and tells you truths you didn't want to hear. The type of growth that doesn't make for a cute Instagram post. The kind that breaks your pride, shatters your excuses, and shows you your own reflection in the mirror of His Word. It doesn't feel like healing, not at first. It feels like conviction, exposure, vulnerability. And if we're honest, most of us came for a hug, not heart surgery.

But let's not get it twisted, conviction is healing. It's the first sign that something in you is waking up, that God isn't ignoring your brokenness but is loving you too much to let you stay broken. It's Him saying, "I see your wounds, and I have the cure. But first, we must clean the infection." And that stings. That burns. That exposes. But it also saves.

The issue isn't that God is cruel. The issue is that we've been misdiagnosed by culture. We're told we're fine the way we are. Those feelings are truth. That we don't need to change, just be affirmed. But the Kingdom of God doesn't run on affirmation; it runs on transformation. You don't get healed by pretending you're already whole. You get healed by admitting you're not and letting the Healer do His job.

In the Faith Clinic, the first thing they do is strip away the fake layers. No titles. No filters. No spiritual resumes. Just you and your condition. You can't skip recovery if you haven't faced your reality. That's what this book is, not a spa day but a surgical table. And you can't afford to flinch now.

Let's talk about expectations. You walked into this book thinking it was going to be a soothing soak for your soul, a few gentle affirmations, a sprinkle of encouragement, and maybe a nice little spiritual "you got this." But surprise! The Holy Spirit doesn't do spa treatments. He does soul excavations. This isn't a eucalyptus-scented devotion with a calming Spotify playlist. This is heart surgery while you're wide awake. And it turns out, God's not interested in just making you *feel* better, He's interested in making you *be* better.

You didn't come to the Faith Clinic for a massage. You came for a diagnosis; one you might not like. And the first tool the Doctor uses? Not a soft towel or a sugar-coated quote, but a mirror. The Word of God isn't always a warm blanket; sometimes it's a scalpel. It cuts past your excuses, slices through your self-preservation, and gets down to the real problem, the infection you've been pretending isn't there. The bitterness you dressed up as boundaries. The fear you baptized as "discernment." The pride you posted online as confidence.

Yeah, we're coming for *all of it*. Because here's the deal: real healing can't happen where fake symptoms are reported. If you only admit surface stuff, "I'm just a little tired," "I need help focusing," "I wish I prayed more", then you'll only get surface-level healing. But if you're bold enough to say what's actually broken, "I'm jealous of everyone around me," "I haven't trusted God in years," "I'm addicted to things nobody knows about," "I use faith as a costume, not a cure", then you're finally able to heal from the *inside out*.

God doesn't fix what you fake. He heals what you reveal. But let me warn you: conviction isn't a vibe. It's not a cute journaling moment. Conviction burns. It's not shameful, but it stings. It wakes you up from spiritual sedation. It opens wounds you swore were "handled." It drags out the secrets that have been making you spiritually sick. It's the moment you realize that you didn't need a day off, you needed an overhaul.

And yeah, sometimes all you're going to walk away with is a Scripture that wrecks your entire mood. A verse that won't leave you alone. One line from Jesus that doesn't comfort you, it confronts you. And that's how you know you're in the right place.

The Faith Clinic isn't about comfort. It's about confrontation, the holy kind. The kind that breaks chains you forgot were still on your ankles. The kind that reminds you that healing isn't a destination, it's a process. And sometimes, that process starts with tears, tension, and telling the truth. So, buckle up. Because what's ahead isn't pretty, filtered, or easy. But it *is* freedom. And spoiler alert: it's worth it.

⚕ FAITH CLINIC INTAKE FORM

Please fill out honestly. God already knows the truth.
Name: _______________________________________

Actual spiritual condition **(circle all that apply):**
☐ Tired of faking it
☐ Emotionally constipated
☐ Can't remember the last real prayer I prayed
☐ On the run from accountability
☐ Here for vibes, not for surgery

Symptoms you're experiencing:
☐ Numbness during worship
☐ Sudden avoidance of Scripture
☐ Mild spiritual rage when someone says "God's timing"
☐ Repetitive sin with a side of shame
☐ Delusions of self-sufficiency

When did these symptoms begin?
☐ After that unanswered prayer
☐ Since I was hurt by *church people*
☐ The moment someone said "God won't give you more than you can handle"
☐ Somewhere between Netflix binges and anxiety spirals

Symptoms (check all that apply):
☐ Spiritually numb
☐ Avoiding prayer like it's jury duty

☐ Worshipping on Sunday, worrying by Monday
☐ Quoting verses you don't believe
☐ Pretending forgiveness while plotting revenge
☐ Secretly resentful of God's timing
☐ Thinking conviction is personal attack
☐ Addicted to busy, allergic to quiet
☐ Reading devotionals, skipping repentance
☐ Serving others, can't stand yourself
☐ Ghosted God, but kept the Christian playlist

When did the pain start?
☐ After the breakup
☐ When the prayers went unanswered
☐ When church became performance
☐ When you finally got what you wanted and still felt empty
☐ All of the above

Do you believe God can heal you?
☐ Yes
☐ No
☐ I want to
☐ Honestly, I'm scared to hope again

List any spiritual allergies:
(e.g. fake people, religious clichés, sermons that avoid real issues)

Have you tried to self-medicate with:
☐ Control
☐ Isolation
☐ Hustle culture
☐ Hyper-religiosity

☐ Netflix and non-accountability
☐ Relationships that feel like therapy but pay in trauma

What are you looking for here?
☐ A miracle
☐ A real encounter with God
☐ Answers
☐ A reason to stay
☐ Permission to leave
☐ Just… something that *feels* like truth again

Do you understand that healing will not be comfortable, quick, or clean?
☐ Yes
☐ No
☐ Willing to try
☐ Only if coffee is provided
Emergency Contact (i.e. the one friend who still calls you out spiritually):
Name: _________________________________
Phone: _________________________________
Relationship: ☐ Real One ☐ Instagram Follower ☐ Pastor Who Knows Too Much

Do you consent to spiritual discomfort, emotional excavation, and a severe lack of sugar-coating?
☐ Yes. (I'm desperate.)
☐ I guess?
☐ As long as it doesn't mess with my schedule.
☐ No, but I'm too tired to argue.

Signature (acknowledging that God is not your emotional masseuse, but your soul surgeon):

Date of your last real encounter with God: _____________

Reflections

____

____

____

____

____

____

____

____

____

____

____

____

____

____

Chapter 1:
Welcome To The Pain Table, This Won't Be Comfortable

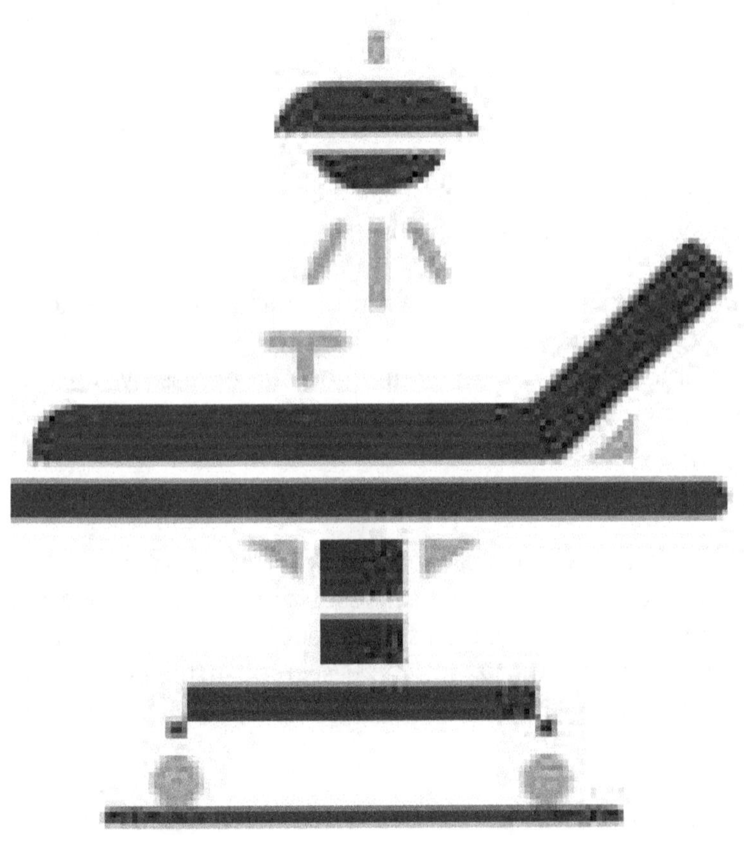

Welcome To The Pain Table

You thought you were walking into a day spa for your soul. Candles, gentle music, a few Scriptures rubbed on your stress like lavender oil. But surprise! You're not here for a massage; you're here for open-heart surgery. Spiritual, emotional, and possibly reputational. This is the table where we don't just get comforted, we get confronted.

See, the Church has done a great job marketing healing. "Come as you are!" we say. But healing isn't just about being welcomed. It's about being changed. And sometimes, change feels like  betrayal to your old self. You didn't sign up for pain, but pain is part of the prescription. Growth requires discomfort. Conviction requires surrender. And transformation? That means something must die, your pride, your excuses, your favorite coping mechanisms.

This is not a vibe. This is not a seven-minute devotion that leaves you feeling encouraged but unchanged. This is invasive. Uncomfortable. Offensive to your ego and necessary for your breakthrough. God's not offering you a warm blanket; He's handing you a scalpel and saying, "Let's cut out the infection before it spreads any further."

This table? It's not where you nap. It's where you wrestle. Where you cry. Where you remember that Jesus didn't die to make your Sundays more palatable, He died so your soul could stop pretending and start healing. It's the table where secrets suffocate and truth perform triage. It's where your filters fail, but your faith might finally breathe.

And maybe that's why you've been avoiding this moment for so long. Because deep down, you knew it wouldn't be pretty. Healing rarely is. But if you've made it to this table, bruised, bleeding, but breathing, then you're already further than most. You're brave enough to stop running and sit with your pain long enough to hear what God is really trying to say.

So welcome. Don't get too comfortable. You're not here to be soothed. You're here to be saved. There are no warm blankets here. No ambient music. No dim lighting and soft whispers. This isn't a massage table for your spirit; this is the *pain* table. Where the soul gets cracked open, the excuses get peeled back, and the infection you've been hiding gets exposed under spiritual surgical lights.

You thought this would be a healing space, and it is. But not the kind you're used to. Not the kind that feels good right away. This is where Jesus flips the table you've been hiding under, points to the scar you won't talk about, and says, *Let's deal with that.* Not the fake pain. Not the church-faced pain. The *real* stuff. The resentment you baptized. The habits you renamed as "personality." The bitterness you justified as boundaries. The trauma you repackaged as testimony without ever actually healing.

This is where your pride gets put under anesthesia. It's uncomfortable here because everything is exposed. The real you, the insecure, doubting, angry-at-God version of you, is on the table. Not the "highlight reel faith" you posted on Instagram. Not the "yes, pastor" version you bring to church. Just *you*. Stripped of titles. Stripped of roles. Stripped off coping. And it hurts. But it's holy.

Because real healing can't begin until your illusions die. The illusion that you've forgiven them. The illusion that you're fine. The illusion that if you serve enough, or pray long enough, or smile big enough, God will overlook the parts of you that are still broken. But He won't. Not because He's cruelled, but  because He *cares* too much to let you stay infected and call it healed.

This chapter is the spiritual equivalent of that sharp inhale you take when the doctor says, "This might sting." You know what's coming.  You want the healing, but not the process. You want resurrection, but without crucifixion. You want growth without pruning. You want change, but only if it doesn't hurt.

Spoiler alert: It's going to hurt. But pain isn't the enemy. Denial is. If you're willing to sit at the table, raw, exposed, trembling in your own uncertainty, then you've already done the hardest part. You showed up. And showing up is the declaration that you believe healing is still possible. Even if you're unsure. Even if you're skeptical. Even if your faith feels like it's hanging by a thread.

You don't need perfect belief to be healed. You just need to stop hiding. God does His best work in exposed places. Broken places. Honest places. And this? You've been avoiding this pain table. It's sacred ground. Because it's where the performance dies, and the real transformation begins.

You walked in for peace, hoping for a scented candle and soft worship music, but instead, the Great Physician laid out a scalpel of truth. No numbing. No Novocain. Just the raw, pulsing pain of conviction hitting places you swore were off-limits. Welcome to the Faith Clinic, where we don't just hand you a warm blanket, we hand you a mirror. And not the cute one from your makeup bag. The kind that reveals wounds you've accessorized, traumas you've spiritualized, and sins you've marketed as personality traits.

This is the pain table. Not a pew. Not a stage. A table where the divine Surgeon gets close enough to cut deep. And no, you don't get to pick the playlist. You don't get to skip your favorite parts. You sit. You squirm. You wrestle. You bleed truth and get stitched together with scripture. Because real healing isn't cozy, it's cutting.

The uncomfortable part is what most people try to pray away. "God, make it easy." But He doesn't do shortcuts. He doesn't believe in Band-Aids over bullet wounds. He takes you all the way in. To that betrayal you never really forgave. To that addiction you renamed as "coping." To that trauma you buried under busyness. He exposes the infection not to shame you, but to save you. And yeah, it hurts. But it's healing, not harm.

Ask anyone who's ever been through real spiritual transformation: there's no glory without the grind. No peace without pressing. No anointing without agitation. We keep asking God to use us, but we resist the sanctification process that makes us usable. So, we showed up to the faith clinic looking for revival, but we skipped the surgery. And God, because He loves you more than your comfort, won't let you bypass the scalpel for a selfie.

You don't grow by being coddled. You grow by being confronted. Jesus didn't walk around Nazareth with spa oils and fluffy robes. He flipped tables. He rebuked demons. He told people to "go and sin no more." If your theology only comforts and never corrects you, it's not biblical, it's bubble wrap.

This chapter is the part of your healing where you start sweating. Where old beliefs twitch on the operating table. Where the Holy Spirit puts pressure on that one thing you swore no one could touch. This is where you ask, "Why does it have to hurt?" And God replies, "Because you keep hiding the wound under religious makeup."

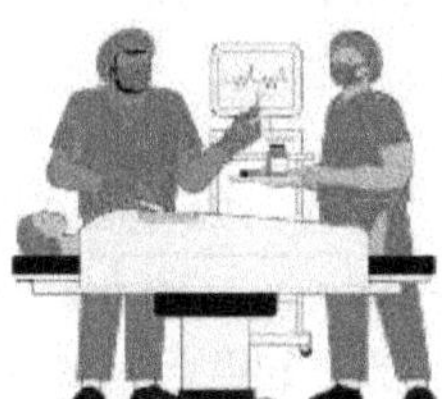

Growth isn't glamorous. Healing isn't always holy-looking. Sometimes it's ugly crying in your car because a sermon hit too close. Sometimes it's confessing sin you tried to spiritualize. Sometimes it's canceling the date with that person you know God said no to three months ago. Welcome to the pain table, where the truth doesn't just set you free, it hurts first.

But you didn't come to the Faith Clinic for comfort. You came because you were tired of fake healing. You came because self-help stopped helping. You came because deep down, you knew something needed to break. That's the good news. God doesn't waste pain. He performs surgery with purpose. And on this table, He's not just removing what's killing you, He's implanting what will sustain you.

You're not here for a temporary fix. You're here for transformation. That's why this table isn't padded, it's purposeful. Because God isn't interested in putting you back together the way you were. He's interested in letting you know. Whole. Free. Unrecognizable to the person you used to be. This is just the beginning.

The Lie Of Soft Christianity

Let's not sugarcoat it: somewhere along the way, we turned the gospel into a TED Talk with coffee and a side of self-care. We rebranded Christianity as a cozy escape instead of a complete transformation. The lie of soft Christianity whispers, "God just wants you happy." And while those sounds comforting on a bumper sticker or TikTok devotional, it's not the gospel, it's a hallucination. Jesus didn't die so we could stay in our comfort zones with curated playlists and good vibes. He came to resurrect the dead parts of us, and resurrection is never painless.

Soft Christianity says, "Come as you are, and stay exactly the same." But the real gospel says, "Come as you are, but don't expect to leave untouched." We've traded in conviction for comfort, sacrifice for self-esteem, and the narrow road for the one that gets the most likes. But here's the hard truth: Jesus didn't come to improve your image; He came to ruin your ego and rebuild your soul.

Youth today are saturated with a message of self-love that often borders on self-idolatry. But what if the love that really changes you comes from laying yourself down, not lifting yourself up? What if healing looks like surrender instead of self-promotion? The gospel isn't an inspirational quote; it's a spiritual surgery. And soft Christianity avoids the scalpel altogether.

There's a version of Christianity floating around that's got more sugar than substance, more affirmations than accountability. It's the kind that promises peace without repentance, blessing without obedience, purpose without pruning. It hands out motivational quotes like vitamins but avoids calling sin what it is, spiritual cancer. This is what we've come to know as *Soft Christianity*, and it's a lie that's been anesthetizing souls in desperate need of surgery.

Soft Christianity tells you Jesus is your life coach, not your Lord. It packages the gospel into ten steps to your best life instead of one radical surrender to the cross. It'll tell you you're already enough but never challenge you to become holy. It's feel-good faith with no fire, no cost, and no cross. But here's the hard truth: if your Christianity has never made you uncomfortable, it probably hasn't made you Christ-like either.

See, this soft version of faith is all about comfort. It teaches believers to pursue God like He's a vending machine, punch in a quick prayer, get out a miracle. But the real gospel doesn't promise ease; it promises endurance. It doesn't start with "you're perfect just as you are" it starts with "repent, for the kingdom of God is at hand" (**Matthew 4:17**). Soft Christianity doesn't prepare you for storms, it just hands you a flimsy umbrella made of clichés.

Let's get even more honest. If Jesus were walking into some churches today, He'd be flipping tables, not handing out lattes. He didn't die so we could be inspired, He died so we could be transformed. There's nothing soft about sweating blood in Gethsemane. Nothing gentle about being whipped until flesh tore off His body. Nothing cute about carrying a splintered cross while people spit in His face. And yet we've tried to reduce His message into a self-help seminar with scripture sprinkles on top.

And the consequences? People walk away when it gets hard. Youth leave the church not because they don't love God, but because no one told them faith would feel like war. They were sold a version of Jesus that came with a refund policy, not a resurrection. So, the moment grief hits, the moment addiction creeps in, the moment the high of the Sunday service wears off, they think something's wrong with them. But nothing's wrong with you. Something's wrong with the diluted gospel you were given.

Jesus said, *"In this world you will have trouble."* (**John 16:33**) That's not a vibe. That's a *guarantee*. But He didn't stop there. He added, "But take heart! I have overcome the world." That's not a motivational catchphrase. That's a war cry. A declaration that no matter how bloody the battle, He's already won it. And we get to walk in that victory, but only if we stop pretending the battlefield is a yoga mat.

Soft Christianity avoids sacrifice. But the real gospel is a call to die daily, to your ego, your pride, your habits, your idols. It's not just about being saved *from* something, it's being saved *for* something. And that something is a life that reflects Christ, not culture. Let's look at Paul. If anyone had an excuse to preach a soft gospel, it was him. He was intelligent, respected, and could've made Christianity sound attractive to the elites of his day. But instead, he said things like, "I die daily" (**1 Corinthians 15:31**) and "I count everything as loss for the surpassing worth of knowing

Christ" (**Philippians 3:8**). Paul didn't hand out cupcakes. He handed out truth, and it got him beaten, jailed, and eventually killed.

Why does that matter to you? Because if you're following Jesus expecting a Pinterest-perfect life, you're going to be confused when all hell breaks loose. But if you know that faith is a fight, that pruning is part of the process, and that conviction is not cruelty, then when the pain hits, you won't quit. You'll dig deeper.

This isn't to say following Jesus is all suffering and no joy, far from it. But it's *joy through the suffering,* not around it. It's peaceful in the storm, not the absence of storms. It's the kind of faith that looks at the enemy dead in the face and says, "You picked the wrong one to mess with today." Not because you're strong, but because He is. And you're rooted, not hyped.

The lie of soft Christianity ends when we stop selling comfort and start embracing the cross. When we stop trying to fit in with culture and start standing out with courage. When we stop watering down the gospel to make it go down easier and start preaching it raw, because that's the only way it heals.

So, if you came looking for a light snack, this might not be your table. But if you come hungry for real change, welcome to the meal that saves souls, even if it burns going down. Because this isn't a spa day for your spirit. This is surgery. And you're going to walk out differently.

Jesus Didn't Promise A Massage, He Promised A Cross

Let's get something straight up front: Jesus didn't come to hand out scented oils and warm towels. He didn't open a healing clinic where the waiting room plays ocean sounds and everyone walks out with a motivational sticker that says, *"I'm blessed and highly favored."* He 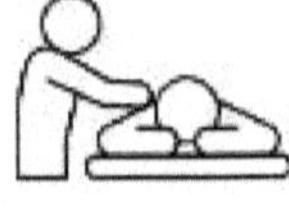

didn't say, "Follow Me, and I'll pamper your feelings." He said, "Follow Me, and *take up your cross*." Huge difference.

This generation, and let's be real, all generations, tends to hear the word "Jesus" and immediately associate it with comfort. Like He's our personal therapist, on-call 24/7, whose main job is to validate our emotions and make us feel better about life. And while yes, Jesus is *compassionate*, and *gracious*, and *tenderhearted*, He is also the same God who flipped tables, rebuked entire religious systems, and told people straight up, "Go and sin no more."

The cross wasn't a spa bed. It was an execution device. A method of public humiliation, agony, and death. And Jesus told us, not asked, *told*, to pick it up. That means following Him is going to *hurt*. Not all the time. But enough that you feel it. Enough that you have to wrestle. Enough that parts of you will have to die so that something greater can live.

We forget how many people *walked away* from Jesus once He started talking about sacrifice. The same crowd that cheered for His miracles turned on Him when He mentioned blood. John 6:66 literally says, "From this time many of his disciples turned back and no longer followed him." Why? Because He said hard things. Like, hard. Things that didn't make sense. Things that didn't feel good. Things like, "Unless you eat my flesh and drink my blood, you have no life in you." That's not exactly the type of message that gets you invited to headline youth conferences.

The modern church often sidesteps the gritty parts of Jesus' message. We create services to be comfortable. We adjust sermons to be palatable. We edit out the offense of the gospel because we're afraid people won't come back next Sunday. But you know what? Jesus was never concerned about *crowd retention*. He was concerned about *heart transformation*.

When Jesus promised eternal life, He didn't do it by saying "Just believe and chill." He made it clear: *believe and die.* Die to yourself. Die to your sin. Die to your pride, your plan, your preferences. **Luke 14:27** lays it out with no filters: "Whoever does not carry their cross and follow Me cannot be My disciple." He didn't say "can't be a *good* disciple." He said *can't be a disciple at all.* So, what does that mean for you, sitting here in 2025, scrolling through your feed, trying to figure out if this Jesus thing is even worth it?

It means He never promised the soft life. He never said you'd always be happy. He never said you wouldn't lose friends, or wrestle with mental health, or battle temptation repeatedly. He never promised you'd be instantly delivered from your addiction or miraculously healed the moment you lifted your hands in worship. But He *did* promise that He'd be with you in the process. He'd carry your shame, your pain, and your story. If you lost your life for His sake, you'd find *it* (**Matthew 16:25**).

That's the beauty and brutality of the gospel; it kills what's fake in  you so the real you can rise. It cuts you before it heals you. It calls you out before it calls you up. Because real growth doesn't come from being coddled. It comes from being *confronted*. And Jesus was, and still is, the most loving confrontational figure you will ever encounter.

Look at His conversation with the rich young ruler. The guy shows up eager, moral, and ready to check off religious boxes. Jesus tells him, "Great, now go sell everything and follow Me." And what happens? The man *walks away sad.* Jesus didn't chase him down. Didn't try to negotiate a lighter version of obedience. Didn't say, "Hey, maybe just tithe a little more and volunteer on weekends."

No. He let the man walk, because you can't follow Jesus and cling to your idols at the same time.

So, why does this matter now, to you, reading this? Because if you don't understand that Jesus *promised a cross*, then when life starts crucifying your expectations, you'll think God failed you. You'll think faith isn't working. But it is. The cross is working. The pain is producing something eternal. **2 Corinthians 4:17** puts it like this: *"For our light and momentary troubles are achieving for us an eternal glory that far outweighs them all."* 

Key word: *achieving*. That means the pain has purpose. The hurt has an agenda.

And don't get it twisted, the cross isn't just about dying. It's also about *resurrection.* But resurrection can't happen without death first. You can't rise if you never fall. You can't be restored if you've never been broken. Jesus doesn't call you to the cross because He wants you to suffer. He calls you to it because He wants you to *live.* Fully. Authentically. Eternally.

So no, Jesus didn't promise a massage. He promised a cross. But He also promised His Spirit, His grace, His strength, and His victory. And when you carry your cross, you're not doing it alone. You're walking the same path He walked, a path that leads through blood but ends in glory. And that's the kind of faith that won't flinch when life hits back. That's the kind of belief that doesn't fall apart when the hype is gone and healing hasn't come yet. That's the kind of Christianity that can stand in a world addicted to comfort and still declare: "Even if He doesn't, I *will* praise Him."

If you came to Jesus expecting a hot stone massage for your soul, surprise: you signed up for crucifixion. **Luke 9:23** says, *"Whoever* *wants to be my disciple must deny themselves and take up their cross daily and follow me.* " Jesus didn't say, "Take up your self-esteem." He said, "Take up your cross." That's not a metaphor for your Monday struggles; that's a call to die to yourself.

The gospel is free, but it will cost you everything. The cross is not a necklace; it's an altar. It's not about getting pampered, it's about getting purified. Real discipleship is a daily decision to crawl up on the operating table of surrender and say, "Cut out what doesn't look like You." And no, that doesn't come with spa music and a calming essential oil blend.

Jesus never promised comfort, He promised presence. And if you follow Him long enough, you'll realize His presence often feels more like fire than feathers. It burns off pride. It scorches self-dependence. It convinces you places you didn't even know were broken. But that's the point. Because on the other side of that fire is freedom. And healing without fire isn't healing, it's a cover-up.

Why Real Healing Is Always Preceded By Real Confrontation

You don't go to the ER and hide your symptoms. You don't walk in bleeding and tell the nurse, "No worries, I just came to chill." And yet, so many walk into the presence of God with hemorrhaging souls and a "just vibes" mentality. We say we want healing, but not the honesty it requires. We want resurrection without burial, restoration without breaking, peace without the process.

But healing, real, gut-level, soul-cleansing healing, doesn't happen on the surface. It begins in the shadowy rooms where truth pulls up a chair and God starts asking questions you'd rather ignore. Like:

"Why do you keep going back to them?" "What are you still angry about from three years ago?" "Why do you need everyone's approval to feel worthy?" That's the spiritual confrontation that precedes any kind of true healing.

Most people want comfort, not confrontation. That's why church-hopping is such a thing. The moment a pastor says something that hits too close to your hidden wound, you're out. The moment a sermon stops feeling like pep talk and starts sounding like heart surgery, you're switching livestreams. But God's love is not a motivational speaker, it's a mirror. And mirrors don't lie. They don't flatter. They show you exactly what needs attention. If you're serious about growth, you'll stop running from the mirror and start inviting the surgeon to work.

Take David, for example. This man committed adultery, covered it up, and tried to move on like everything was cool. Then God sent Nathan, the prophet, not with a hug, but a confrontation. Nathan told David a story that exposed the ugliness in his heart. That wasn't a feel-good devotionality was divine intervention. And David's response in Psalm 51 gives us the blueprint for healing: "Search me, O God… create in me a clean heart." Notice: David didn't ask for a better image, he asked for a new heart. That's the difference between spiritual survival and spiritual healing.

Today's culture celebrates your truth, your vibe, your journey—but what about *His truth*? Real healing requires aligning your wounds with His Word. And that's not always pretty. Because the Word of God isn't a soft blanket, it's a sword (**Hebrews 4:12**). It cuts. It divides. It exposes motives, attitudes, and all the subtle self-deceptions that keep your bound. But that pain? That discomfort? That's the anesthesia-free surgery of grace.

You'll never change what you're still coddling. Some of us are stroking our trauma like pets, rehearsing old heartbreaks like monologues, and defending our dysfunction as personality traits. But God's not trying to hurt you, He's trying to free you. Confrontation isn't cruelty; its kindness wrapped in truth. It's the doctor saying, "This cancer must go. And yes, the surgery will be painful, but living without it will kill you."

So, let's stop running from the hard conversations. Let's stop ghosting accountability. Let's stop glamorizing the pain we were meant to heal from. Real healing confronts. Real healing convicts. Real healing requires you to look God in the face and say, "I'm ready to stop hiding. Do what You need to do." Because here's the truth: healing is always a side effect of surrender. And surrender starts when you finally let God address the part of you you've been pretending wasn't sick.

We love the idea of healing until we realize it requires confrontation.  Healing starts with the Holy Spirit flipping on the fluorescent lights in your soul's exam room and saying, "Let's talk about this." And suddenly, you're squinting at areas you've avoided for years: bitterness, insecurity, addiction, lust, anger, fear. God doesn't do band aids, He does biopsies.

You can't be transformed by a truth you're unwilling to confront. **John 8:32** doesn't say, "The truth will coddle you." It says, "The truth will set you free." But before truth liberates you, it will first offend you. It will slap the spiritual sleep out of you and force you to deal with the stuff you've been suppressing behind spiritual quotes and "I'm fine" smiles.

God won't heal what you refuse to expose. You can't ask Him to fix what you're still pretending isn't broken. That's why the first step in the faith clinic isn't a prescription, it's an X-ray. God holds up your soul to the light and says, "Let's get real." And yes, it hurts.

But it's the hurt that leads to hope. Because He doesn't confront to shame you, He confronts to free you. Let's just go ahead and ruin the fantasy right now: healing isn't cute. It's not a montage of spa music, bubble baths, and Bible journaling with pastel markers. Healing, real, biblical, rip-you-open-and-rebuild-you heal, starts with confrontation. Not with your friends. Not with your ex. With *you*. It starts when God holds up the mirror and you don't recognize the person looking back, because the real you have been buried under layers of trauma, excuses, and well-practiced church behavior.

Here's the raw truth nobody wants to put on an inspirational quote graphic: You can't heal what you won't admit is broken. And you *can't* fix what you're still pretending doesn't hurt.

That's why Jesus, the Great Physician, doesn't start with a soothing balm. He starts with a scalpel.

Think about the woman at the well in John 4. She came to the well thinking she was just going to get water. Jesus met her there and within minutes, He was cutting straight into the wound. "Go call your husband." Bruh. She didn't ask for therapy. She didn't come for a counseling session. But Jesus wasn't offering water for her *thirst*. He was offering water for her *truth*. And before He could pour in healing, He had to expose where she was still bleeding.

That's confrontation. And it's not to shame you. It's to *save* you.

See, conviction isn't God yelling at you. It's God loving you loud enough to tell you the truth. It's Him pointing to the thing that's killing you and saying, "This has to go if you're going to grow." He does it with the tenderness of a surgeon, not the rage of a critic. He doesn't call you out to punish you. He calls you out to *pull you out*, of the cycles, the lies, the numbness, the fake peace that's just emotional avoidance dressed up in Christian language.

You know how many people show up in prayer asking for healing but just want validation? They say, "God, make me whole," but what they mean is, "God, make me feel good without having to face myself." But God is not a genie. He's not interested in making you feel better for ten minutes. He's interested in making you whole for a *lifetime*. And that starts with confrontation.

Even David, the man after God's own heart, didn't get healed from his moral collapse until the prophet Nathan came with that iconic line: "You are the man." Not in a motivational sense, in a *you're-the-one-who-just-wrecked-your-own-life* sense. Psalm 51 was born *after* that confrontation. And it remains one of the rawest confessions of repentance and healing we've ever read.

David didn't find healing in the palace. He found it in the place of being exposed. And that's where a lot of us are stuck. We want restoration but not repentance. We want wholeness but not honesty. We say we want freedom, but not if it costs our image, our comfort, or the narrative we've created to justify our dysfunction. But God loves you too much to let you heal wrong. 

Because false healing is dangerous. It creates people who *look* okay but are emotionally infected beneath the surface. It builds churches full of people who shout during praise breaks but won't admit they're still harboring bitterness. It turns small groups into performance spaces and prayer meetings into pitiful parties. And none of that leads to lasting freedom.

You can't cast out what you won't confess. James 5:16 puts it plainly: "Confess your sins to one another and pray for one another, so that you may be healed." Not forgiven, *healed*. Because confession isn't just about morality; it's about medicine. It's the spiritual equivalent of saying, "Hey, I've got this gash and I've been covering it with a nice shirt and pretending I'm fine, but I'm actually bleeding out."

Confession is confrontation's best friend. It takes courage to say, "This is what's really going on. This is where I keep falling. This is what I've been hiding." But that courage unlocks healing. That honesty makes space for God to do what only He can.

And if you don't believe confrontation is a gift, remember this: Jesus confronted Peter too, after Peter denied Him three times. Jesus didn't cancel Peter. He called him deeper. But not before asking three painful, exposing, repeating questions: "Do you love Me?" Not because Jesus didn't know the answer. But Peter needed to hear the question *until the wound gave way to healing*.

That's what Jesus still does today. He sits you down. Looks you in the eye. And says, "Let's deal with that." Not to break you down, but to break the chains. Not to embarrass you, but to remove the infection. Not to punish you, but to perform soul-level surgery that Instagram quotes and avoidance can't fix.

So, if you're feeling uncomfortable, convicted, exposed, congratulations. That means the healing has already started. Welcome to the table. This won't be comfortable. But it *will* be worth it.

The Waiting Room Of Conviction

There's a strange in-between space that no one talks about, not in Sunday sermons, not on social media devotionals, and not on those shiny church flyers with 

the happy, smiling stock photos. It's called the *waiting room of conviction.* It's the spiritual equivalent of sitting in a hospital gown under fluorescent lights, knowing something's wrong, but you haven't seen the doctor yet. You're not sure how long it'll take, but you do know one thing: you're not leaving this place the same.

This is where conviction lingers, and healing hasn't quite landed.

Some people mistake it for punishment. Others try to rush through it like it's a DMV line. But the waiting room isn't where you're forgotten; it's where you're *facing yourself.* And if you sit there long enough, still, honest, open, you start hearing God clearer than ever.

Because conviction isn't just about feeling bad. It's about feeling *awake.*

You start realizing that the noise you've drowned your life in, the scrolling, the busyness, the fake busy-ness, can't mute what God is whispering now. "You can't carry this into your next season. You're bleeding out under that outfit. You're not okay, and that's where I meet you."

The waiting room strips you. It strips of your titles. Your habits. Your polished "I'm fine" face. It exposes your pain in the most sacred way. You're left alone with God, your thoughts, and the ache of truth that doesn't let you go back to how things used to be.

Let's pause here for a moment, because for some of you reading this, *this* is where you are right now. You're not partying. You're not prospering. You're *processing.* You've come face-to-face with the realization that you've been functioning wounded. That your smile is more script than sincerity. That you've been asking for revival while living on autopilot. And now, the Holy Spirit has gently (or not-so-gently) put His finger on the exact thing that needs to be addressed. That's conviction.

It's like sitting in the ER, not because you want to be there, but because you finally *can't ignore the pain anymore.* The prodigal son had this moment too. Long before he ever made it back home, he had to sit in the pigsty of his decisions and say the words, "I've sinned." Nobody gave him a revival playlist. Nobody handed him a robe yet. There was no "suddenly" miracle moment. Just a boy, a mess, and honesty that maybe, just maybe, he needed to go home, even if it meant limping back with nothing but shame and repentance.

But let me tell you what that waiting room *does* promise. It promises that you're still *reachable.* Still *teachable.* Still *loved.* Because if you can feel conviction, that means your heart isn't hardened. That means you haven't silenced the Spirit. That means God's hand is still on you, and He's not done pulling you out of whatever pit you've been pretending isn't real.

Some of the most powerful moments in your life won't happen at an altar or in a crowd. They'll happen right here, in the quiet, holy space between "I'm not okay" and "I'm ready to change." That's the miracle of the waiting room. It doesn't offer instant results. But it offers access. Access to repentance that restores you. Access to truth that sets you free even before the breakthrough happens. Access to the kind of healing that rewires how you think about yourself, your patterns, and your purpose.

Don't try to decorate this space. Don't try to escape it. Don't slap a Bible verse on the wall and call it healing. Let the process you. If the Holy Spirit is confronting you, let Him. If He's asking you questions you've been dodging, don't log off. Sit there. Be still. Let the ache become an altar.

Remember, it was in the *stillness* that Elijah heard the whisper. Not the fire. Not the earthquake. But the still, small voice that knew his name and his fears.

You're not alone in this waiting room. Heaven is leaning in. The Great Physician hasn't forgotten you. He's just preparing the operating table. So, take a breath. Wipe your tears. And stay long enough to let the conviction finish what it started. Healing is coming. But not before *honesty*.

This is where most people get stuck, the divine holding area where God has shown you what's wrong but hasn't yet pulled it out. Welcome to the waiting room of conviction. It's uncomfortable. It's quiet. It's that space between "I know I need help" and "I'm ready to surrender." It's the moment before the surgery where the Spirit asks you to sign the consent form.

Conviction is not condemnation. It's clarity. It's when God starts revealing patterns, cycles, and infections that have been silently robbing you. Maybe it's the fake friendships you keep avoiding being alone. Maybe it's the way you use your body to get attention. Maybe it's the religious mask you wear so no one sees your doubt. Whatever it is, conviction brings it to the surface, not to shame you, but to offer you a chance to heal.

Hebrews 12:11 puts it like this: *"No discipline seems pleasant at the time, but painful.*

Later, however, it produces a harvest of righteousness and peace."* The waiting room doesn't feel good, but it's necessary. Because conviction is proof that your heart is still soft enough to be shaped.

And if you're feeling the weight of it now, congratulations. That means God is still calling, still caring, still committed to your recovery. So, sit in the waiting room if you must. Cry if you need to. But don't run. Because of the pain, your feeling isn't punishment, it's preparation. And the Surgeon is already scrubbing in.

The Pain Table Is Sacred, Even If It Feels Like Punishment

The first thing you need to know is this: pain is not always punishment. But in the faith world, we've made it out to be. If something hurts, we assume we're in trouble. We ask God, "What did I do wrong?" as if discomfort is divine disapproval. But that's not what Scripture teaches. Sometimes, pain is the very evidence that something is healing. It's not a sign of abandonment. It's the mark of attention.

Hebrews 12:11 (NIV) reminds us, *"No discipline seems pleasant at the time, but painful. Later, however, it produces a harvest of righteousness and peace for those who have been trained by it."* Let that sink in. Pain is not the enemy; untrained pain is. When you refuse to learn from your wounds, they rot. But when you let God train you through them, they become part of your harvest. Your trauma doesn't just get recycled, it gets redeemed.

Some of the deepest growth happens not when you shout your faith, but when you whisper your surrender. Not when you post Scripture to look spiritual, but when you kneel beside your bed and say, "God, I'm tired, and I don't know how to keep pretending I'm fine." The pain table is where the pretending stops and the processing begins.

God Isn't Afraid Of Your Blood

You might be thinking, "Yeah, but if God really saw what I've been through, what I've done, He wouldn't want anything to do with me." First off, He already saw. And He still showed up. Jesus was never squeamish around the bleeding, the broken, or the bitter. Think of the woman with the issue of blood (**Mark 5**). She had been bleeding for twelve years, cast out by her community, labeled unclean. But when she touched Jesus, He didn't recoil, He responded. He didn't lecture her. He called her "Daughter."

Your bleeding doesn't disgust God; it draws Him in. But you must get close enough to let Him do the work. Stop settling for religious spectatorship when what you need is divine surgery. The altar isn't a place to pose; it's a place to bleed safely.

Don't Mistake Numbness For Peace

Here's the trap: many of us have confused numbness with peace. You've shut down emotionally and called it "trusting God." You avoid vulnerability and call it "strength." You suppress your tears and label it "faith." But God doesn't heal what you won't reveal.

Peace is not the absence of emotion. It's the presence of God in the middle of your emotion. True peace lets you cry and still believe. It lets you be confused and still move forward. It's not denial, it depends on it.

John 14:27 (NIV) says, *"Peace I leave with you; my peace I give you. I do not give to you as the world gives. Do not let your hearts be troubled and do not be afraid."* Jesus wasn't promising the peace of avoidance, He was offering the kind that coexists with your trembling hands and uncertain heart. That's the kind of peace available at the pain table, but only if you're honest enough to admit you need it.

The Cost Of Not Healing Is Higher Than The Cost Of Confrontation

Let's be honest. Sitting at this table costs something. Your comfort. Your convenience. Your coping habits. But the cost of staying broken is higher. It'll cost you your joy, your clarity, your ability to love fully. Avoiding pain never makes it go away; it just buries it under layers of behavior you don't even recognize anymore.

Maybe you're short with people because you've been wounded by betrayal and never forgave. Maybe your silence in prayer isn't discipline, but distance. Maybe your hustle is hiding your hurt.

Psalm 34:18 (NIV) says, *"The Lord is close to the brokenhearted and saves those who are crushed in spirit."* But some of us are so busy avoiding being brokenhearted that we miss the nearness of God entirely.

Your Pain Has A Purpose, But Not Until You Give It To The Surgeon

Your story, as messy and jagged as it may be, holds the potential to be a ministry. But it can't be used if it's still infected. God can use anything, even your lowest moments, but first, He wants to heal them. He wants to remove the bitterness, the fear, the lies you picked up along the way. He wants to sterilize the wound so that what comes out of you next isn't just survival, but revival.

This won't happen in one service. Or one therapy session. Or one conversation. It's a process, painful, personal, and holy. But it starts here. On this table. With your truth. With your surrender. With your willingness to be undone so God can rebuild you for real.

Final Words Before The First Cut

This is your moment. The lights aren't dimmed. The music isn't playing softly. This is raw, real, and unfiltered. You came looking for healing, and instead you're being handed conviction and Scripture. Not because God's cruel, but because He's kind. Kind enough to give you what you need instead of what you wanted.

This chapter was never about comfort. It was about courage. The courage to stay in the seat. The courage to trust the hands of the

Surgeon. The courage to believe that even this, the breaking, the weeping, the trembling, is the beginning of becoming whole.

So, if your hands are shaking right now, good. That means you're alive. That means you're still capable of being transformed.

Welcome to the Pain Table. This won't be comfortable, but it will change your life.

Chapter 1 Reflection: Soul Check-In

Before you flip the page and march confidently into Chapter 2, pause here. This is your post-surgery moment. You're still on the table. You're not bleeding out, but you're not skipping out of the clinic yet either. This reflection is your chance to check the X-rays of your soul and acknowledge what just got cracked open.

- *What part of this chapter was exposed to you the most?*

____

____

____

- *What truth did you resist at first, but now realize you needed?*

____

____

____

- *Have you bought into a "soft gospel" that comforts but never corrects?*

____

____

____

____

____

- *Are you avoiding the cross Jesus called you to carry?*

____

____

____

____

____

- *What part of your healing do you still pretend that you don't need confrontation?*

____

____

____

____

____

Write it down. Pray it out. Let discomfort do its job. You came for healing, but healing doesn't happen through hiding.

Now take a breath, because the next chapter is not the waiting room. It's the **operating room**.

Chapter 2:

Open Heart Surgery, Cutting Through the Numbness

Let's get something straight: numbness isn't peace. And just because you're not screaming in pain doesn't mean you're healed. Some of us aren't healthy, we're just heavily sedated by distractions, spiritual avoidance, and religious routine. We don't feel God not because He left, but because our hearts are so wrapped in bandages of self-protection that His touch can't even get through.

Chapter 2 is where the scalpel hits the scar tissue. We're not diagnosing symptoms anymore. We're cutting into causes. This is the part of the clinic where anesthesia isn't an option and pretending doesn't work. You're not dead, but parts of you are spiritually paralyzed. Jesus doesn't do surface-level healing. He touches the core, the wounds from childhood, the betrayals that twisted your theology, the prayers you stopped praying because you didn't like His timing. And He's not afraid to dig until the infection is gone.

So, let's be honest: You don't need another motivational post. You need heart surgery. And the Great Physician isn't here to impress you. He's here to fix you.

Let's begin.

When Spiritual Numbness Becomes Your Default Setting

You didn't just wake up numb one day. It was a slow fade. A gradual silencing of your spiritual pulse. One day you were praying with fire and feeling like God Himself was holding your journal. The next? Silence. Blank pages. Empty words. It's not that you don't believe anymore, it's that you don't *feel* anything anymore. And you've become strangely okay with that.

Spiritual numbness is like frostbite of the soul. At first, it's painful. You feel the sting. The coldness of disconnection. You know something is wrong. But after a while, the pain fades… and that's when it gets dangerous. Because numbness isn't the absence of pain, it's the warning that something deeper is dying quietly.

Somewhere between the fake "I'm fines and the robotic church routines, your heart checked out. You went from worship to performance. From prayer to parroting. From passion to pretending. And nobody noticed, not even you, until the hollowness got too loud to ignore.

The problem with spiritual numbness is that it doesn't announce itself. It doesn't kick in the door with chaos. It seeps in with subtle disinterest. You stop reading. You stop praying. You stop caring. And you don't even fight it. You just drift into apathy.

And let's be honest, numbness feels safe. After all, pain is exhausting. Disappointment with God? That's hard to sit with. Praying and feeling ignored? Who wants that? So, you slip into emotional autopilot. And suddenly, numbness becomes your coping mechanism. But here's the danger: what protects you from feeling also blocks you from healing.

Jesus never invited us to be emotionally neutral. He wept. He flipped tables. He grieved. He sweated blood. That's not emotional numbness, that's divine humanity. And you? You were never called to be a robot. You were made to feel deeply, to believe passionately, to ache righteously.

The good news? Numbness doesn't mean you're faithless. It means you need surgery not punishment. You need the Great Physician to touch what went silent. To warm the parts of you that froze during heartbreak. To revive the heart that stopped hoping because hope started to hurt too much.

Ezekiel 36:26 says, *"I will give you a new heart and put a new spirit in you; I will remove from you your heart of stone and give you a heart of flesh."* That's not just poetic, it's surgical. God specializes in heart transplants. But He can't operate on what you keep covering.

So, what's the first step? Honesty. Raw, uncomfortable honesty. The kind that says, "God, I don't even want to want You right now." Or "I'm scared to feel again because last time I did, I got wrecked."

That's not rebellion. That's surrender. That's letting the Healer in. Spiritual numbness is curable, but not by pretending it's not there. It's healed when you let Jesus bring sensation back to your soul. And yes, it might hurt at first. But it is better to feel pain than to stay dead.

How Conviction Shows Up In Your Habits, Not Your Hashtags

It's one thing to post a Bible verse. It's another way to live like you read it. We live in a generation where it's easier to curate spirituality than to cultivate it. We know how to hit "share" on a highlight reel of scriptures, but behind closed doors, our daily routines are spiritually bankrupt.

Conviction, though? Real conviction doesn't matter what your social media bio says. It shows up in your choices, your patterns, your little daily "yeses" and "nos." It's the way you shut off the toxic show when no one's watching. It's how you apologize for real, not for likes. It's what keeps you humble when your flesh wants to be petty.

Conviction is God's kindness, not His condemnation. It's not Him yelling from a pulpit; it's Him whispering in your routines. You feel it when you scroll too long. When you ghost God but somehow keep texting that person who pulls you further from Him. You feel it when your playlist is a vibe but your soul gets numb to filth. Conviction shows up when your actions don't match the faith you pretend to wear like a hoodie.

Hebrews 12:11 says, *"No discipline seems pleasant at the time, but painful. Later, however, it produces a harvest of righteousness and peace for those who have been trained by it."* That's the fruit of conviction. Peace and righteousness, not punishment. Conviction isn't about shame. It's about realignment.

Let's be honest: spiritual maturity doesn't scream through megaphones. It whispers through consistency. Your habits matter more than your highlight reel. Conviction turns into fruit when you let it shape your schedule, not just your Sunday.

Here's how you know conviction is working: you start making micro-shifts. You don't need a sermon to tell you what's off, you just feel it in your chest. That awkward "don't go there" in your spirit. That quiet "choose better" before you send the text. That "you're better than this" voice when you want to spiral.

This isn't about perfection. This is about alignment. Conviction gets louder when you're out of step with God's rhythm. And the more you obey it, the easier it becomes to follow. Like spiritual muscle memory. But ignore it too long? You build scar tissue around your soul, and eventually, what once made you pause no longer makes you flinch.

The Spirit of God isn't trying to micromanage you. He's trying to raise you. Conviction is evidence that you're loved, not abandoned. It's the inner nudge that says, "I see where this is going… let's take a better route." So, stop measuring your faith by how many Christian influencers you follow. Start measuring it by the fruit your daily life is producing. **Galatians 5** doesn't mention "having a cute Jesus Pinterest board." It talks about love, joy, peace, patience, kindness, goodness, faithfulness, gentleness, and self-control.

You want to know if God's working in your life? Check your habits. Check your default reactions. Check the little decisions you make when no one's watching. That's where conviction shows up, not in your hashtag game, but in your obedience when no one's clapping for it. Because spiritual growth isn't aesthetic. It's obedience when it's inconvenient.

Soul Check: Is It Conviction Or Condemnation?

Ever felt like trash after a church service or Bible study? Not the holy "I need to get right" kind of heavy, but the "I'm the worst human alive and God is probably done with me" kind of weight? Yeah, that's not conviction. That's condemnation wearing a Sunday sweater and faking a holy accent.

Let's be clear: conviction and condemnation are not twins. They're not even cousins. They may sound alike and show up to the same places (like your devotional time or during that worship song that hits too hard), but they come from totally different parents. Conviction comes from God. Condemnation comes from the enemy. One leads to healing. The other leads to hiding. So, here's your soul check: which voice are you listening to? Conviction says: *You messed up, but you can still come home.*

Condemnation says: *You are the mess, and you'll never belong again.* Conviction is the gentle scalpel of the Spirit cutting away what's killing you. Condemnation is a chainsaw swinging wildly, trying to destroy what God's still building in you.

Romans 8:1 says it best: *"Therefore, there is now no condemnation for those who are in Christ Jesus."* If you're in Christ, you're not living under a spiritual eviction notice. You're not being threatened with disqualification every time you fail. You're being discipled, not dismissed.

But let's not confuse conviction for comfort. Real conviction can *sting.* It presses into the parts of your personality you like to hide behind. It taps on your habits, not your hashtags. It's not out to cancel you, it's out to **call you back**. Conviction says, *This is not who you are. Let Me remind you who I made you to be.* It doesn't throw your past in your face to shame you; it shines a light on your present so you can walk forward.

But how do you tell the difference in real time? Here are some signs:

- **Conviction draws you closer to God.** Even if you're embarrassed or broken, you feel that tug to pray, to repent, to come home.
- **Condemnation drives you away.** You avoid God, you ghost your Bible app, and you convince yourself He's probably just tired of forgiving you.
- **Conviction gives you a clear next step.** Apologize. Fast. Forgive. Delete the app. Call your mentor. It leads you somewhere.
- **Condemnation paralyzes you.** You sit in shame, replay the mistake, isolate, and silently self-sabotage.

And if you're wondering which one's louder, it's almost always condemnation. The enemy is *obnoxious*. He knows if he keeps the same playlist on repeat in your head, you won't even *try* to hear God's grace. Here's the thing: the devil doesn't just want to tempt you; he wants to torment you after you give in.

Conviction is from the same Spirit that raised Jesus from the dead (**Romans 8:11**). That's not a spirit of shame. It's a spirit of **resurrection**. It speaks about life, not labels. It calls you out *so it can call you up.*

Let's pause and check our soul with some real talk:
- Are you replaying your failure more than you're rehearsing God's promises?
- Are you more familiar with guilt than with grace?
- Have you stopped praying because you think He's mad, not because you're busy?

God's not passive-aggressively ignoring you because you slipped up. He's still the Father from Luke 15, the one who *ran* when His son came limping home, smelling like pigs and shame. He didn't even let the prodigal finish his speech. That's what conviction does, it cuts through the excuses and wraps you in mercy before you can finish disqualifying yourself.

You don't need to live under the weight of a "not good enough" mentality. That's not holy, it's hellish. It's not reverence, it's religion. And Jesus didn't die so you could live in a guilt loop. He died to break it.

If you've been walking around in spiritual rags, believing you're too broken, too dirty, too much *whatever*, hear this: ***Conviction doesn't disqualify you, it delivers you.*** It reminds you that there is a better way, a higher path, a healed version of you that's not just possible, but promised.

So, the next time you feel that heaviness after a hard work or a hard moment, ask: *Is this pulling me into God or pushing me away from Him?* That answer will tell you everything you need to know about whether it's the Spirit's scalpel or the enemy's chains.

Conviction = Invitation.
Condemnation = Isolation.

And your soul deserves to know the difference, because one leads to wholeness, and the other will keep you spiritually bleeding on a hospital bed you were never meant to die on.

There's a fine line between conviction and condemnation, and most  of us have crossed it unknowingly while dragging our shame behind us like it belongs. You ever feel like every time you try to do better; there's a voice in your head screaming, "Too late!" or "You always mess up anyway"? That's not Jesus. That's condemnation. And there's a huge difference.

Conviction is surgical. It cuts to heal. Condemnation is blunt force trauma; it beats you down to paralyze. Conviction says, "Hey, this isn't right, let's fix it." Condemnation says, "You're not right. You're broken. Stay down."

Romans 8:1 makes it plain: *"Therefore, there is now no condemnation for those who are in Christ Jesus."* That verse isn't saying you'll never feel bad about sin. It's saying God doesn't shame His children into growth, He leads them through it with grace.

Here's the heart check: if what you're feeling leads you to repentance and peace, that's conviction. If it leads you to shame, avoidance, anxiety, and quitting, condemnation at the wheel.

The enemy is the accuser. Jesus is the healer. That matters. Conviction will highlight your misstep. Condemnation will try to convince you that the misstep defines your identity. Conviction exposes sin. Condemnation tries to cancel your worth. Conviction corrects you because of your value. Condemnation crushes you and whispers that you never had value to begin with.

In real life? Conviction makes you want to lean into accountability, into scripture, into grace. Condemnation makes you hide. Avoid church. Dodge your prayer closet. Turn out the people who care. It creates spiritual isolation and calls it "figuring it out on your own." Meanwhile, you're slowly ghosting God.

Let's talk about the silent treatment some of us give God after we sin. That weird shame-driven silence? That's condemnation pretending to be humility. It's like saying, "God, I know You're forgiving but let me punish myself a little longer." As if your guilt is holier than His grace. Let's shut that down right now.

You are not the exception to God's mercy. There's no asterisk next to your name in heaven. God didn't say, *"My grace is sufficient... unless your mistake was extra embarrassing."* Nope. He said, *"My grace is sufficient for you, for My power is made perfect in weakness"* (**2 Corinthians 12:9**).

Conviction might sting, but it always leads to healing. Condemnation feels like drowning in guilt with no hand reaching out. It's that voice that says you should stop trying because you'll never get it right. But God is the one saying, "Get up. Let's try again. I'm still here."

One of the biggest lies we believe is that God gets tired of us needing grace. That somehow, we've exhausted our "free refills" of mercy. But **Lamentations 3:22-23** tells a different story: *"His mercies are new every morning."* Every. Morning. Not just on the days you're proud of yourself. Not just when you finally journaled or didn't mess up. Every. Morning.

So, next time your soul starts spiraling into self-hate because you messed up again, paused and asked: Is this conviction or condemnation? Because God's voice won't contradict His character. He corrects, but He doesn't crush. He disciplines, but He doesn't disown. If what you're feeling drives you *away* from God, that's not Him talking. That's a counterfeit gospel, one rooted in fear, not love. Remember, Jesus didn't come to rub your sin in. He came to rub it out.

Let that truth reshape your recovery process. You're not climbing out of guilt to earn back God's love. You're walking in conviction *because* you already have it.

When God Puts His Finger On What You're Avoiding

You know that one area of your life you keep dodging? The one you casually skip over in prayer like it didn't happen or doesn't hurt? Yeah, that one. God's not ignoring it, He's waiting for you to stop pretending it's not bleeding.

God is not passive about your healing, but He is patient. He waits for the moment you stop covering the wound with excuses, distractions, or fake strength and finally say, "Okay, God. Let's deal with this." He puts His finger on the tender spot not to expose you but to treat you. Think of it like this, no good surgeon ignores the exact place of injury. They press. They examine. They isolate the source of the pain. And yes, it stings. But it's necessary for targeted healing.

God's version of this? It shows up in sermons that feel oddly specific. In conversations that hit too close to home. In quiet moments when the Holy Spirit whispers, "We still haven't talked about *that* yet." It's no coincidence, it's divine precision. Some of us treat spiritual healing like a buffet, we pick and choose what parts of our life we want God to touch. "Fix my finances, Lord, but don't touch my relationships." "Teach me purpose, but don't make me forgive." "Bless me, but don't break me." And yet, true healing demands surrender.

 The hard truth? The longer you avoid what God is trying to address, the more infected it becomes. Avoidance delays freedom. That hidden hurt, that unconfessed sin, that unresolved bitterness, it's not dormant. It's *festering*. God doesn't heal surface wounds with surface prayers. He goes deep. And when He places His finger on something, it's an invitation to wholeness, not a setup for shame.

Let's be honest. Most of us *know* what God is asking us to confront. It's the relationship you know isn't healthy. The lie you keep living. You downplay the addiction because it's "not that bad. The bitterness you wear like armor so you won't feel vulnerable again.

But here's the good news, God never presses His finger on pain without the intention to apply His hand for healing. He wounds only to mend. As Hosea 6:1 says, *"Come, let us return to the Lord. He has torn us to pieces but He will heal us; He has injured us but He will bind up our wounds."*

So how do you respond when God highlights what you've buried? First: stop hiding behind "I'm still processing." Healing and honesty go hand in hand. Yes, the process is real. But sometimes what we call processing is just polite procrastination.

Second: invite God into the exact area you're avoiding. Not the cleaned-up version. Not the edited-for-prayer-group version. But the ugly, raw, confused, and real mess.

Third: remember, obedience in the area God is pointing to will unlock healing in places you didn't even know were broken. What if your peace is on the other side of surrender? What if your clarity is connected to the thing you refuse to face?

When God calls something out, it's not to embarrass you. It's to *extract* the poison. The longer you keep numbing it, the longer you delay the healing. One of the boldest prayers you can ever pray is this: "God, show me what I'm avoiding." It's terrifying. It's vulnerable. It's surgery-level soul work. But it's worth it.

Because at the end of the day, God isn't trying to take something *from* you, He's trying to heal something *in* you. And the truth is, He'll keep circling back to it. Because that's what love does. Love doesn't leave you stuck. Love doesn't settle for surface survival. Love brings truth, even when it's uncomfortable. So let Him in. Let Him press. Let Him heal.

⚕ Faith Clinic Reflection Page

Patient Name: ___________________________________

Date of Visit: ___________________

Spiritual Condition: ☐ Stable ☐ Fragile ☐ Avoidant ☐ "Don't Ask"

⚕ Diagnostic Questions For The Soul

1. **What area of your life are you pretending is "fine" but needs healing?**

    (Be honest. God already knows anyway.)

2. **What emotion do you avoid feeling because it exposes pain you haven't processed?**

    ☐ Guilt

    ☐ Shame

☐ Fear

☐ Anger

☐ All of the above

Explain:

3. **What is one repeated habit or relationship that may be a symptom of spiritual numbness?**

4. **When was the last time you asked God to show you what you're avoiding?**

Date: _______________________________

What did He show you?

5. **Do you know the difference between conviction and condemnation in your life?**

6. Condemnation keeps you hiding. Conviction invites you into healing. Which one have you been living under?

☐ Conviction

☐ Condemnation

☐ I don't know

Explain why:

⊘ Prescription for the Week

- **Prayer Prompt:**
  "Lord, shine Your light on the things I've been trying to hide. I don't want to numb it anymore; I want to heal."

- **Scripture to Meditate On:**
  "Search me, God, and know my heart; test me and know my anxious thoughts. See if there is any offensive way in me and lead me in the way everlasting." **Psalm 139:23–24 (NIV)**

- **Challenge:**
  Tell one trusted spiritual friend the area God is putting His finger on. Confession isn't a weakness; it's your treatment plan.

- **Reflection Goal:**
  By the end of this week, be able to name the wound… and invite God to work on it.

REFLECTIONS

____

____

____

____

____

____

____

____

____

____

PERSONAL NOTES

Chapter 3:

"Stop Praying For Band-Aids When You Need Surgery"

This chapter is for the believer who keeps asking God to make things "go away" instead of allowing Him to go *in*. It confronts the tendency to pray vague, comfort-based prayers instead of submitting to deep spiritual transformation.

It's raw. It's messy. And it's necessary. Because sometimes, you're not just bruised, you're broken. And broken things can't be fixed with motivational quotes and microwave devotionals.

Your Soul Doesn't Need A Quick Fix, It Needs A Full Procedure

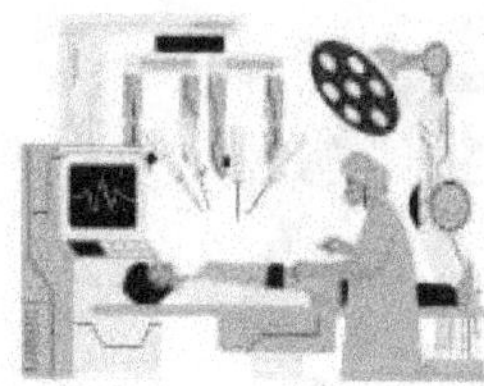

Let's just go ahead and admit it, we live in a microwave culture trying to serve a Crock-Pot God. We want everything instant: instant peace, instant answers, instant purpose. We scroll past videos if they're longer than 60 seconds and tap out of conversations the moment, they get "too deep." Unfortunately, that same expectation has bled into our spiritual life. We show up at the altar like it's a drive-thru: "Hi God, yeah I'll take one answered prayer, peace of mind, and maybe some healing on the side, and could You please make it fast because I have anxiety and a soccer game at five?" But the truth is: your soul isn't a light switch that can be flipped into wholeness. It's a surgical case. And you can't heal what you won't let God cut open.

There's a massive difference between *relief* and *recovery*. And many of us are only asking for relief. Relief says, "Make the pain go away." Recovery says, "Make me whole again, even if it hurts first." One is rooted in comfort. The other is rooted in surrender. But here's the hard part: true spiritual healing will never cater to your comfort zone. It will call you into the operating room, ask you to lay down your pride, your defense mechanisms, your curated Instagram spirituality, and let God begin to remove what's killing you from the inside out.

This is why so many young people feel like "church didn't work" or "God didn't fix it." It's not because He didn't show up, it's because we kept asking Him to do a Band-Aid blessing when He's trying to do open-heart transformation. We pray prayers like, "Lord, just help me get through this week," when what we really need is to say, "Lord, expose what in me keeps sabotaging my own peace." One leads to temporary relief. The other leads to permanent restoration.

Look at King David. When he messed up, and we're not talking a small mistake, we're talking full-blown sin with a woman who wasn't his wife, followed by murder, his prayer wasn't, "God, just help me feel better." It was "Create in me a clean heart, O God, and renew a right spirit within me" (**Psalm 51:10**). David wasn't just asking for forgiveness. He was asking for a *procedure*. He knew what we often forget that sin leaves soul damage. And soul damage requires more than a good cry during worship and a "this too shall pass" pep talk. It requires spiritual operation.

Maybe you've been asking God to just "fix things" in your life, but deep down, you know the problem is deeper than the symptoms. You don't need God to fix your grades, your dating life, or your anxiety alone. You need Him to pull out the roots that keep producing insecurity, fear, anger, and self-hate. That means getting into the operating chair and telling the Great Physician, "Do what You have to do, even if it breaks me before it builds me."

This is the part nobody tells you about healing: it doesn't feel holy at first. It feels humiliating. Because when God starts cutting away your coping mechanisms, you start realizing how much you depended on the fake stuff just to survive. The fake peace, the fake confidence, the fake relationships, the fake strength. You realize how long you've been living with infection in your spirit but covering it with "I'm fine."

Let's talk about the word, *infection*. In the medical world, when something's infected, you can't just cover it and hope it goes away. That's how people lose limbs. That's how people die. Spiritually, it works the same way. When you keep covering trauma with distraction, pain with perfectionism, or shame with silence, you don't get healed, you get *sicker*. And before you know  it, what started as a small wound becomes an identity. That's why God doesn't just want to touch you. He wants to *open* you.

Cut. Cleanse. Stitch. Restore.

This process is never glamorous. But it's always worth it. Jesus didn't come to be your therapist; He came to be your *Savior*. He doesn't hand you coping strategies and hope you figure it out. He gets in the mess with you, calls out what's been lying to you, and performs heart surgery right in the middle of your breakdown.

And maybe you're wondering, "Why can't God just snap His fingers and fix me?" The answer is love. Love doesn't force healing. Love invites participation. God is not a dictator with a scalpel; He's a Father with hands that know how to mend. But He won't force you on the table. That's your choice. Healing always starts with surrender. And surrender always starts with honesty.

So, before you ask God to "bless this mess," maybe start by asking Him to *clean it out*. Open the prayer journal. Tell Him what hurts. Invite Him into the ugly. And when the cutting begins, the conviction, the confessions, the spiritual stretching, don't tap out. Stay on the table. You may walk out of this with some soul stitches, but you'll also walk out free. Because here's the truth, no one puts on a T-shirt: *Healing hurts before it helps.* But it helps in ways nothing else can.

Anesthesia Won't Work On What You Keep Numbing

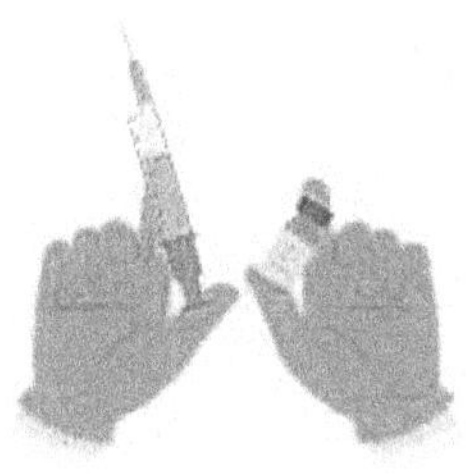

You ever try to go numb on purpose? Of course you have. We all have. You ghost your group chat. You binge-watch three seasons of a show you barely care about. You scroll TikTok till your thumb cramps. You pretend it's "just been a long week" when really, your soul has been on silent mode for months. And while numbing can feel like control, it's just avoidance in a prettier outfit.

Here's the truth: you cannot heal what you refuse to feel. And you cannot feel what you've trained yourself to numb. We live in a generation that runs from discomfort like it's the plague. We don't sit with pain; we scroll past it. We don't wrestle with conviction, we mute it. But the problem with emotional anesthesia is that it doesn't just dull the pain, it dulls *everything*. Joy. Love. Faith. Truth. When you go numb, you don't get to choose what you shut off. It's all or nothing.

Spiritually, this kind of numbness is lethal. You start mistaking silence for peace. You start thinking "I'm not crying anymore" means "I'm better now." But numb isn't healed. It's paused. And if you don't press play again, if you don't open yourself back up to feel, God's healing won't go deep enough to last.

Paul didn't say, "Be chill in the Lord always." He said, "Rejoice in the Lord always" (**Philippians 4:4**). Rejoicing is an emotion. It's not surface-level. It comes from a heart that *feels* deep. David wasn't numb. This man wrote entire Psalms sobbing, raging, repenting, dancing. He felt it all. And it's because he felt it that God could *heal* it.

Here's the issue though: many of us are asking God to move in our lives without giving Him access to our insides. It's like showing up to surgery and refusing anesthesia *and* refusing to let the surgeon cut. We don't want pain, but we also don't want to be vulnerable. We don't want brokenness, but we also don't want God to touch our broken parts.

So, what do we do instead? We self-medicate. We numb with likes, followers, fast food, flirting, caffeine, overachievement, fake peace, and too many late-night "just checking in" texts from people we don't even like. Because staying busy is easier than being broken. But here's the real problem: numbing works…until it doesn't.

Eventually the pain you keep pushing down will push back harder. The emotions you've been ignoring will burst like pipes. The spiritual exhaustion will catch up to your body, your relationships, your mental health. The lie that "you're okay" starts sounding hollow even to you. You're spiritually dizzy, emotionally drained, and you're wondering why God "feels distant" when the truth is: He's been speaking, you've just been sedated.

And this is where God does His best work, not in the highlight reels, but in the confession rooms. Not when you've got it together, but when you finally say, "God, I've been trying to fix myself with feelings, distractions, and fake smiles, and I'm still a mess." It's in that raw, unfiltered moment where you stop numbing and start kneeling that healing begins.

Let's talk biblically. The woman with the issue of blood had spent everything she had on physicians, every earthly method, every worldly fix. But her healing came when she finally reached for Jesus (**Luke 8:43–48**). She had to get past the crowd. Past the embarrassment. Past her "I'll handle it myself" mentality. And that's what you'll have to do too.

You can't numb and receive at the same time. You can't live off spiritual anesthesia and expect resurrection power. Resurrection comes *after death.* After pain. After surrender.

And here's what might mess you up, in the best way: God is not afraid of your feelings. Not your sadness. Not your rage. Not your questions. Not your spiritual exhaustion. He doesn't require you to "be okay" before He starts working. He just requires honesty. Remember, even Jesus wept (**John 11:35**). Even Jesus sweat drops of blood from stress (**Luke 22:44**). So why do we think spiritual strength means emotional silence?

You may think you're protecting yourself by numbing. But you're

actually robbing yourself of the most intimate encounters with God. It's often in the moments when you're too tired to fake it, too broken to filter it, and too desperate to care how you sound, that's when Heaven invades. That's when God bypasses your performance and meets you in your pain.

Here's what I need you to understand: God will not force Himself past your numbing habits. He's not going to pry your phone out of your hand, force you to pray, or make you cry on cue. But the moment you open the door, even a crack, He'll step in with grace that breaks through the fog.

So, if you're numb today, don't shame yourself. Just *notice it.* And then start the slow process of coming back to life. One prayer at a time. One journal entry. One honest moment. One worship song where you listen instead of just letting it play in the background.

Stop trying to feel spiritual and start being honest. Tell God, "I don't know what I feel. I don't even know what to pray. But I don't want to be numb anymore." That prayer alone is powerful enough to crack open what you've been protecting for too long. Because the truth is: God can't heal what you won't hand over. And healing doesn't start with fireworks. It starts with *awareness*. With choosing to wake up. And trusting that even though you may feel nothing now, you won't feel this way forever.

Numbness is not your identity. It's the season. And the Great Physician knows how to bring you back from it, if you'll let Him. Have you ever had a Soul X-Ray? I have. It is simply letting the Word of God read what you've been hiding.

So, let's be honest, you've got stuff buried. Deep. Not just the "oops, I slipped up last weekend" kind of stuff. We're talking about the fears, the cycles, the bitterness you've baptized in spiritual lingo so no one must call it what it is. You might not even remember what the root pain is anymore, you've layered it with enough sermons, "I'm fine" responses, and a highlight reel of faith-y sounding tweets to make it disappear. But the truth is, it's still there. It's just hiding better than before.

Enter the soul X-ray: the Word of God. **Hebrews 4:12** says it plain: *"For the word of God is alive and active. Sharper than any double-edged sword, it penetrates even to dividing soul and spirit, joints and marrow; it judges the thoughts and attitudes of the heart."*

If that doesn't sound like divine surgery, I don't know what it does. The Word doesn't just observe you. It opens you. It reads your motivations, dissects your rationalizations, and shines light into corners you forgot even there. And here's what we usually do instead: we read it like a checklist instead of letting it check us.

We don't come to scripture to *be seen*; we come to *look spiritual*. But this book, this ancient, breathing, divine diagnostic tool isn't a motivational quote generator. It's a mirror, and not the Instagram-filter kind. It's not here to flatter you. It's here to free you. But let's talk about why we avoid this X-ray in the first place: because we know what it might show. We're afraid it'll call out that jealousy we keep dressing up as ambition. That people-pleasing we've renamed "servant leadership." That addiction we've hidden under the guise of "stress relief." That relationship we say is "missional" when it's messy and misaligned.

The truth? God's Word doesn't need your PR spin. It's not asking you to come perfectly, it's inviting you to come open. It doesn't shame you; it scans you. Not to condemn, but to cleanse. Think of David in **Psalm 139**. The man literally prayed, *"Search me, God, and know my heart; test me and know my anxious thoughts. See if there is any offensive way in me and lead me in the way everlasting."* That wasn't a passive scroll through Proverbs. That was David crawling up on God's X-ray table and saying, "Show me what I can't see, even if it hurts."

That's what real healing takes. Vulnerability.

The problem is, we treat scripture like it's a vending machine. "Let me press A3 for encouragement. B7 for forgiveness. Skip the repentance section, I'm not in the mood today." But scripture is not your snack bar. It's a scalpel. And it's coming for your infection, not just your symptoms.

Let me be real: the Word is not always comforting. Sometimes it convicts you so hard, you sit in silence afterward like you just got spiritually slapped. And that's a *good* thing. Because a God who only comforts you but never corrects you isn't a good Father, He's a co-signer in your dysfunction. And the Word is not here to cosign your comfort. It's here to confront the cancer in your soul.

You know what's wild? We trust doctors to put us under anesthesia, slice us open, and rearrange our insides, all because they've got a certificate and a white coat. But when the God of the universe, the One who literally wrote the manual on your life, tries to diagnose you through scripture, we ghost Him. Why? Because it's easier to keep pretending, you're okay than admitting you need divine surgery.

Let's bring it closer: Have you ever had a verse read you so hard,  you slammed your Bible shut like it betrayed you? Yeah, that's the X-ray doing its job. That's not condemnation. That's correction wrapped in divine love. Because conviction is proof that you're still spiritually alive. You see, numbness isn't fixed by more noise. It's fixed by revelation. You don't need louder music, another YouTube sermon, or a more hype church service. You need the quiet, invasive whisper of God's Word reading you back to life.

You need verses that make you pause. Psalms that make you weep. Gospel stories that unearth the parts of you that still haven't come under grace. You need the Book to do what it was designed to do, expose you, in love. This is how soul healing starts: not by running to more Christian content, but by letting the content of the Word *run through you.*

Now, practically, how do we do that? You stop reading for information and start reading for transformation. That means, instead of asking, "What does this mean?" you start asking, "What in me needs to change because of this?" You stop rushing your time with God and start inviting Him to sit with you in the tension. You read slowly. You read repeatedly. You let one verse wreck your schedule if it needs to. You pray dangerous prayers like, "God, if there's anything in me that's off, put Your finger on it, even if I've been ignoring it for years." And then, you sit still and listen. You let the Word name your defense mechanisms. You let it label your anxiety, your pettiness, your pride. You let it cut through the chaos of your mind and call you back to the truth.

Because here's the paradox: God's scalpel is the safest blade you'll ever face. It cuts to heal. It wounds to save. It is open to set free. And if that sounds scary, it's because it *is*. But it's also the most freeing thing you'll ever experience.

So, the next time you feel the urge to numb, to scroll, to zone out, to avoid, crack open that Bible like it's the X-ray of your soul. Let it pierce. Let it speak. Let it break and build you at the same time. Because of the real miracle? Aren't that God reading your mind, it's that He *lets* you read His Word. And in doing so, He offers to heal what you've been hiding.

Surgical Silence is Learning to Hear God in the Quiet of Conviction. It's funny how silence can feel louder than a room full of chaos. You know the type, the awkward, soul-thick quiet that hits right after you pray and… nothing. No thunder. No goosebumps. No signs. Just air. Maybe a flickering lamp if you want to get dramatic. Welcome to the surgical room of conviction, where God says more with His silence than most people do with a podcast.

Let's talk about it: silence isn't absence. It's precision. Ever been in surgery? Probably not while fully awake (and if you were, you're owed several apologies). But here's the thing: when a surgeon is operating, it's quiet. Why? Because everyone in that room knows they're not there for small talk, they're there for transformation. Every move is intentional. Every silence is full of focus. The scalpel isn't loud, but it's doing holy work. So is God's silence.

We live in a generation where noise is medicine, or at least a numbing agent. If a moment gets too quiet, we fill it. Music. Netflix. A scroll through someone else's life. TikTok theology. But conviction often doesn't shout, it settles. It creeps in when your playlist ends and your thoughts get loud. When the car's quiet after church. When you're brushing your teeth and your heart gets heavy out of nowhere.

God is the only one who can say everything without saying a word.

Some of us think He's ghosting us when really, He's guiding us through the hush. His silence is not a punishment; it's a pause that prepares your ears for the next command. Because let's be real: most of us don't *listen* to God, we just wait for Him to say what we already agree with. But in the silence, He doesn't coddle your preferences. He confronts your patterns. And that's where the real spiritual surgery begins.

Think about Elijah. Dude just called fire down from heaven. Epic moment. 10/10 prophet behavior. But then he runs, hides, and wants to die. God finds him in a cave (the Bible's version of emotional rock bottom) and tells him to stand on the mountain because His presence is going to pass by.

Cue the theatrics: a powerful wind, an earthquake, fire, but God isn't in any of those. And then? A whisper. A still, small voice (**1 Kings 19:11–12**).

Why whisper? Because God wasn't just showing Elijah power. He was having heart surgery. When you're whispering to someone, they've got to get close. They've got to learn in. They've got to *focus*. That's the invitation of conviction; it doesn't force itself; it waits for you to come closer. To still your soul. To stop scrolling. To shut up long enough for your spirit to finally start listening.

God whispers not to hide but to heal. So, if your spiritual Spotify is on pause and heaven feels like it hit "Do Not Disturb," don't assume you've been abandoned. Assume you're being prepped. Because conviction doesn't always feel like fire, sometimes it feels like silence, and stillness, and surgical still moments that slice straight through your soul's surface.

Let's get practical. What does it look like to hear God in the quiet?  It looks like reading scripture and asking God to highlight what *you've been ignoring*. It looks like journaling without editing yourself. It looks like confessing the thought before you've figured out how to fix it. It looks like letting tears fall before you rush to apologize for your pain.

Conviction comes when you let your spirit stop performing. Maybe you've been talking *at* God instead of talking *with* Him. Maybe you've been begging Him to show up in fire, but He's been whispering through fatigue. Through that relationship that ended for your protection. Through the guilt that won't let go until you confront what's underneath it.

And here's a truth for someone who's tired of praying and hearing nothing: God's silence doesn't mean He left the room. It might just mean He's already spoken, and now He's watching to see if you'll move on what He already said. That old text He sent you, the scripture you've bookmarked but not obeyed. Yeah. That one. Sometimes conviction isn't a new word, it's the echo of an old one you haven't responded to yet. So, here's the dare: get quiet enough to hear the knife.

Let the silence work on you. Let the Word you avoid reading you. Sit with that verse until it offends you and then ask why. Let conviction teach you how to breathe again. Because real faith isn't built on constant noise, hype, or perfectly curated church moments.

It's built in the quiet trust that God is working even when He's whispering.

Surgical silence is scary. But healing is hiding in the hush. And if you'll sit still long enough in the operating room of conviction, you'll find that the God who seems silent is speaking in scalpel strokes, not to shame you, but to save you.

God Doesn't Do Surface Work, He Cuts To The Core

Let's just go ahead and say it: God isn't interested in your spiritual skincare routine. He's not applauding your "highlight reel holiness" or throwing blessings at your filtered faith. This isn't a cosmetic clean-up. It's *surgery*, and He's not stopping at the surface.

The moment you check into the Faith Clinic, God doesn't come in with a self-care basket. He shows up in surgical gloves. Because what's broken isn't just your behavior, it's deeper than that. It's that scary tissue from when they left you. It's a spiritual infection from trauma that was never treated. It's the pride you covered with praise hands. And let's be honest, it's ugly, uncomfortable, and not "Sunday shareable."

But here's the deal: God doesn't flinch. He sees right through your "I'm good, just busy" mask. He looks past the "Bible verse in my bio" performance. And while you're begging Him to just fix the symptom, the addiction, the insecurity, the anxiety, He's already reaching for what's *underneath it*. That root you've been watering with excuses. That bitterness you've spiritualized. That childhood wound that grew into adult walls. Gods after that.

Because real healing starts when the wound is exposed, not when it's hidden behind spiritual cosmetics. **Hebrews 4:12 (NIV)** says, *"For the word of God is alive and active. Sharper than any double-*

edged sword, it penetrates even to dividing soul and spirit, joints and marrow; it judges the thoughts and attitudes of the heart." Let's sit with that: *It penetrates.* Not *touches.* Not *glances off.* Not *applaud your effort.* It *cuts through everything.* Soul and spirit. Joints and marrow. Heart and hustle. And that's where most of us tap out, right?

We like a Jesus who comforts our pain, not one who exposes what's feeding it. We want Him to remove the thorn; not open the flesh to see how deep it's gone. We want peace, but we don't want *to process.* But what if your breakthrough isn't in bandage, but in the blade?

What if God's cutting is kindness? The enemy wants you numb, distracted, fake smiling your way through spiritual gangrene. But God? He puts His hand right on the infection and says, *This needs to come out.* Not because He's mean. Not because He's disappointed. But because He's the only one willing to go that deep and stay there until it's clean. And can we talk about how this shows up in real life?

- You prayed for peace, but God brought up your unforgiveness.
- You asked for a new relationship, and He resurfaced the last one you never healed from.
- You wanted a platform, and He took you back to the pride you've been hiding under perfectionism.
- You begged Him for clarity, and He brought you into *silence* so He could detox your dependence on everyone else's opinions.

This isn't punishment. This is *precision.* Because the soul doesn't heal through spiritual sedation. It heals through sacred surgery. Ask anyone who's walked with God for real, there's always a moment when you realize He's not just changing your situation. He's changing *you*. From the inside out. Not repainting your brokenness but reconstructing it.

And here's where it gets real: God's cuts often feel like loss before they look like love.

- Losing the relationship that was sabotaging your identity.
- Walking away from the group chat that feds your insecurity.
- Giving up the spotlight because it fed your ego more than your faith.

But here's the gift: He doesn't cut to harm. He cuts to heal.

You are not being punished. You're being purified. That sharp word from a sermon? That stinging truth during your quiet time? That moment in worship when you broke into tears for no reason. All scalpels in the hands of the Great Surgeon. You don't need more confirmations. You need an operation.

You don't need another motivational post. You need a move of God that gets in between your fake and your freedom. You don't need surface-level safe space. You need a holy space where God says, *I'm getting that infection out today. I love you so much to let it spread any further.* And yes, it's scary. Yes, it's intimate. Yes, it costs comfort. But the recovery is worth it. Because when God gets to the core, He rewrites the script. Not just behavior modification, but heart transformation.

Ezekiel 36:26 (NIV) says, *"I will give you a new heart and put a new spirit in you; I will remove from you your heart of stone and give you a heart of flesh."* That's what He's after. Not your performance. Not your Pinterest spirituality. Your *heart*. Soft. Open. Responsive. So, the next time you feel like He's "doing too much," remember: the surgeon isn't being extra, He's being exact. And your healing isn't just about what you *feel*. It's about what He's *fixing*.

Let Him cut. Let Him go deeper. Because you won't find full healing while you're still negotiating surface-level solutions. The Great Physician doesn't miss. And He doesn't waste a single incision.

Surgical Silence, Learning to Hear God In The Quiet Of Conviction

It's not just quiet. It's *too* quiet. Like the awkward, humble kind of silence you feel in the exam room when the doctor walks in, reviews your chart, and doesn't say anything for a minute. You start sweating, overthinking. You wonder what's wrong. You want answers, and all you get is stillness. That's how God sometimes works when He's about to go *in,* not with noise, but with *needles-down* stillness.

Welcome to the part of the healing process that doesn't trend on Christian TikTok.

There are no fireworks here. No catchy conference worship songs.  No back-to-back miracles flooding your inbox. Just... silence. No divine "downloads." No goosebumps. Just the Surgeon of Heaven standing over your soul in complete quiet, gloves on, eyes focused, heart tender, hands holy. And here's the thing no one tells you: *silence is a surgical sound.* Heaven isn't ghosting you. God's not giving you the cold shoulder. He's clearing the room for deep work.

See, when you're in surgery, the room has to go quiet. Distractions get removed. No unnecessary movement. Everyone focused. The atmosphere shifts from casual to critical. And sometimes, that's exactly what God is doing with your life, silencing the noise so He can save the *soul.* But we panic, don't we? We assume the silence means He left us. We mistake stillness for absence. We think quiet equals punishment, when it often means *preparation.*

Lamentations 3:26 (NIV) says, *"It is good to wait quietly for the salvation of the Lord."* Let that sink in *good... to wait... quietly.* Yeah, that's not exactly our vibe, right? We live in a generation that refresh apps every 10 seconds for new notifications. We don't do silence. We fill it. We scroll on it. We numb it. But what if what feels like God's silence is His *scalpel* working?

Let's talk about what silence is really doing:

- **It exposes what you've been depending on.** When the music stops and your favorite preacher's not preaching and the Instagram algorithm's not sending you one-liners from heaven, can you still sit with Him? Can you still listen when He's not shouting?
- **It reveals your idols.** Silence has a way of smoking out what we've secretly been worshipping. Your schedule. Their approval. Your own voice. The feeling of always being "used by God" instead of simply *being with* God.
- **It deepens your discernment.** Conviction isn't always loud. Sometimes it's a slow, seeping sense that something is off. Not dramatic. Not thunderous. Just a steady hand pointing at the infection beneath your smile.

Because conviction doesn't need volume to be *valid.*

Let's break a myth quick: God isn't louder when you're better. He's not quieter because you messed up. He's *consistent,* but our ability to hear changes when we're detoxed from noise, pride, and distraction. Here's a hard truth: Sometimes God must let you sit in the silence long enough for your fake strength to run out.

When your routines stop working. When your formulas stop producing. When you realize that what you called "faith" was just emotional momentum. And it's in that moment, when you finally shut up and show up, that God begins His deepest work.

Ask Elijah. That prophet had just called down fire from heaven in a spiritual mic drop. But one Jezebel tweet later, he's hiding in a cave, begging to die. And God? He doesn't yell. He doesn't thunder. He doesn't burn down the cave. He comes in a whisper.

1 Kings 19:11–12 (NIV) says, *"The Lord was not in the wind... not in the earthquake... not in the fire. And after the fire came a gentle whisper."* Why? Because God knows what every skilled surgeon knows: sometimes the most critical incisions happen in silence. You don't need volume, you need *vision*. You don't need noise, you need *nearness*. You don't need constant reassurance; you need *root work*.

Let me say this to the one who's in that quiet place right now: You're not being ignored. You're being *inspected*. God isn't passive. He's precise. He's digging beneath the surface of your wounds, your patterns, your spiritual facades. And that work can't be done in a concert crowd or a spiritual high. It's done in sacred silence.

And here's what happens on the other side of it: *you learn to hear Him with your life, not just your ears. You start noticing how conviction feels like holy tension, not toxic shame. You start recognizing His presence in moments that don't look "anointed" like folding laundry while forgiving your past. You begin to associate His voice with stillness, not just hype.*

This is the surgery you didn't ask for, but it's the one that saves you. The Faith Clinic isn't interested in numbing your dysfunction. It's after *healing*. And that healing requires you to stop feeling the silence and start *feeling it*. Because some of the most divine downloads you'll ever receive won't come through a microphone, they'll come in the moments you didn't hear anything... but *know* you were being held.

So, let the silence do its work. Let it whisper what shouting never could. Let it cut what clamor could only cover. Because when it's quiet, the lights are low, and the distractions are gone, that's where healing begins. Not with volume. But with vision.

Scars Are Proof That Surgery Worked, Stop Hiding Them

Let's get this straight, a scar isn't a shame. It's a survival story. And if you've ever been through anything real with God, anything painful, gut-wrenching, or faith-challenging, then chances are you've got some spiritual scars too. Not the kind you flex on Sunday with a cute testimony and a filtered smile, but the kind that still sting a little when someone asks, "What happened to you?"

We live in a culture that celebrates the glow-up but avoids the scary story. We're all about the comeback, but allergic to the confession. We posted the healing but hid the surgery. But hear this: in the Kingdom of God, your scars are not liabilities, they are living proof that *the procedure was successful.*

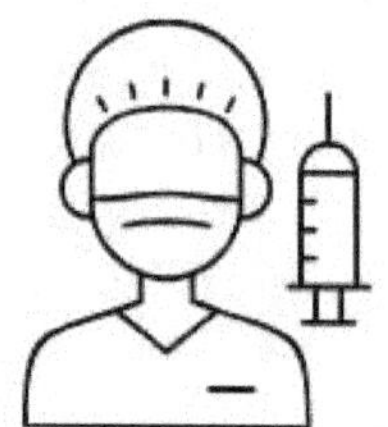

Every healed place came with a wound. Every deep prayer came from a broken place. And every true testimony started with *trauma*. Why? Because real healing costs something. It costs pain, time, surrender, obedience, and a willingness to let God cut away what's killing you, pride, addiction, bitterness, insecurity, codependency, or whatever your soul was clinging to survive.

But let's be honest: most of us don't want anyone to know we were ever *that* broken. So, we cover. We filter. We spiritualize. We become experts in "blessed and highly favored" lingo, when deep down, we're just *barely hanging on.* It's time to flip that narrative. **John 20:27 (NIV)** shows us what Jesus did with His own scars: *"Then He said to Thomas, 'Put your finger here; see My hands.*

Reach out your hand and put it into My side. Stop doubting and believe.'"

Jesus didn't hide His scars. He *showed them.* Not because He needed validation. Not because He was stuck in the pain. But because He knew that someone else's faith depended on seeing that the wound didn't win. That's what your scars can do, too. When you stop hiding your story, you become a living, breathing example that healing is possible. You become a *billboard* of grace. Not perfection. Not performance. Just *proof.*

But here's the kicker: to show the scar, you must *have the wound.* You must admit that the surgery was necessary. You have to confess that you were bleeding emotionally, mentally, spiritually, and that only the Holy Surgeon could stop the hemorrhaging. That's vulnerable. That's messy. That's real. And that's exactly what this generation needs.

This generation is not impressed by churchy cliches and holy camouflage. They don't want your filtered faith. They want to know: *Did it work for you when life broke you? Did God hold you when everything else let you go? Did healing change you? Did the cut heal clean?*

And if the answer is yes, then stop tucking that scar away like it's a secret. Stop spiritual gatekeeping your testimony like it's a VIP-only story. Because someone's sitting in the same operating room you once survived, and they need to know it's possible to walk out whole.

Your scar could save someone else's life. Your "me too" could be the difference between someone giving up or holding on. Your visible healing could become their invisible hope. We weren't meant to be a church of people pretending we were never wounded. We were meant to be a *recovery center* where scars are celebrated as signs of life.

Think about the woman with the issue of blood. She didn't get healed until she pushed through the crowd, *with her mess, with her shame, with her bleeding still happening.* Jesus didn't turn her away because she was still messy. He didn't disqualify her because her issue was public. In fact, her healing became public *on purpose.*

Luke 8:47 (NIV) says: *"Then the woman, seeing that she could not go unnoticed, came trembling and fell at His feet. In the presence of all the people, she told why she had touched Him and how she had been instantly healed."*

Did you catch that? She told the story *in the presence of all the people.* She didn't get to heal and run. She had to reveal and reclaim. That's what showing your scars does. It doesn't just free you, it helps others recognize the surgeon. It says: "Look what grace stitched together." It says: "Here's what He did for me, and He can do it for you, too."

But let's also be real: not everyone will applaud your healing. Some people will still want to treat you like the person you were before the surgery. They'll still call you by your addiction, your past, your trauma, your worst mistake. That's okay. You don't show your scars to *them.* You show them to the one who's bleeding in the same place you once were. You show them because silence doesn't heal shame, *testimony* does. You show them because transparency breaks cycles that secrecy preserves. You show them because Jesus bled publicly so we could heal *boldly.*

So, here's your prescription today:

- Show the scar.
- Name the place He stitched you back together.

- Honor the places you almost didn't make it out of.
- Speak life to the person still in the ICU of their soul.
- Refuse to glamorize the pain, but don't hide the proof of healing either.

Because every scar is sacred. It means something tried to destroy you and *failed.* It means God's grace went deeper than the damage. It means your story didn't end in the middle of the mess. It means you are not what happened *to* you, you are what was healed *in* you. And listen, this world doesn't need perfect people preaching from ivory towers. It needs *real ones*, willing to roll up their sleeves, point to the scar, and say: "This is where He found me. This is where He healed me. This is what's possible when you let Him cut the infection out."

So, stop hiding. Stop dressing your wounds with pride or silence or shame. The scar *is* the testimony. It doesn't mean the pain didn't happen, it means *it didn't get the final word.* Let the world see the Surgeon's work. Let the scar speak.

Let's dismantle the lie right now: scars aren't signs of failure; they are signatures of survival. In a world obsessed with image, perception, and keeping the pain neatly tucked behind a polished exterior, scars make people nervous. They force us to acknowledge that healing is messy, growth is painful, and the journey with God is rarely clean-cut. But spiritual maturity doesn't look like flawlessness, it looks like faithfulness in the aftermath of breaking. Every scar you carry is not a reminder of weakness, but of divine intervention.

Scars don't lie. They don't filter the pain or gloss over the process. They are brutally honest. And maybe that's why we've grown so uncomfortable with them, because in church culture, vulnerability is often mistaken for weakness, and healing gets wrapped in platitudes instead of process. But here's the truth: if your faith has never been wounded, it probably hasn't been tested. If your soul has never been cut open by conviction, it probably hasn't been truly surrendered. And if you're hiding every healed place like a secret, you're missing the chance to help someone else survive their storm.

We've glamorized the highlight reel and sanitized the testimony. We tell people about the mountaintop but skip the details of the valley. We talk about resurrection power but leave out the three days in the tomb. But what if your greatest ministry isn't your platform, it's your scar? What if your most powerful sermon isn't spoken, it's seen on the place where you almost gave up, and God pulled you back together?

Jesus didn't hide His scars.

That's the part that wrecks me every time I read **John 20:27**: "Then He said to Thomas, 'Put your finger here; see My hands. Reach out your hand and put it into My side. Stop doubting and believe.'" He didn't say, "I'm over it now." He didn't say, "Let's not talk about what happened." He showed the marks. Why? Because Thomas didn't need a lecture. He needed proof. Tangible, touchable, undeniable evidence that Jesus really went through it and came out alive. And so do the people around you.

Your family doesn't need your Instagram devotionals; they need your honesty. Your friends don't need another motivational quote; they need your testimony. Your generation is drowning in curated spirituality and performance-based identity. They don't need fake perfect people pretending they never got wounded. They need real ones who are brave enough to say, "This is where I bled. This is where I broke. And this is where grace met me."

Let's talk about the woman with the issue of blood. Scripture says she bled for twelve years. Not twelve hours. Not twelve days. Twelve years of hiding from shame, of spending everything she had on healing that never came. And when she finally touched Jesus, she didn't slip away unnoticed.

Luke 8:47 (NIV) *says, "Then the woman, seeing that she could not go unnoticed, came trembling and fell at His feet. In the presence of all the people, she told why she had touched Him and how she had been instantly healed."* Jesus allowed the healing to be public because the story wasn't finished without the testimony.

She could have gone home, healed and quiet. But instead, her scar became a story, one that validated the power of faith and the nearness of Jesus. And here's the key: she didn't wait until everything looked perfect to speak. She told it while trembling. While still shaken by the experience. While still unsteady. And yet, her courage to be honest freed more than just herself, it freed every onlooker who'd been suffering in silence. Your scars have a similar assignment.

But let's be clear, showing your scars is not about rehashing pain for attention. It's not trauma porn. It's not spiritual exhibitionism. It's stewardship. It's saying, "This is where I saw God up close. This is where I thought I'd die, but He sustained me.

Let me see if I can say this in a different way. Let's get something straight right now, a scar is not a blemish. It's not imperfection. It's not something you should shrink back from or strategically cover with spiritual concealer. It's a badge of survival, a signature from the Healer Himself that says, "I was there. I cut it out. I closed it up. And this child lived." That scar you keep trying to hide. It's not shame. It's a story. And more importantly, it's a sermon someone else desperately needs to hear.

This generation is walking around with soul wounds they've been told to cover, conceal, or clean up before they can be used by God. We've glamorized the "after" photos in our testimonies but buried the bloody mess that came before the miracle. And so now, we've got a church full of people thinking healing means hiding, wholeness means spotlessness, and holiness means fake smiles and silence about the struggle. But Jesus never taught us to fake healed. He taught us to show the proof.

Let's go back to the Gospel of **John, chapter 20, verse 27**. Jesus had just risen from the dead, the greatest miracle of all time, and when He shows up to prove His identity, He doesn't come through with fireworks or lightning. He shows His scars. To Thomas, the doubter, the struggler, the realist who needed to see something tangible to believe, Jesus says, "Put your finger here. Look at My hands." Pause. The resurrected Son of God still had scars.

He could've come back flawless. Could've shown up in resurrected glory without a trace of trauma. But He chose to keep the scars. Not because He was still hurting, but because someone else needed to see them to believe.

That's you, too.

Someone else is looking at your life right now, scrolling through your filtered photos and polished prayers, wondering if God really heals like you say He does. And here you are, with a backstory that could break chains and a scar that could spark faith, but you're hiding it because somewhere along the way you believed the lie that healed people aren't supposed to look like they've been through anything.

But in the Kingdom, scars don't disqualify you. They validate you. At that moment you walked through depression and came out still breathing? Scar. That season you relapsed but came back stronger? Scar. That heartbreak that almost ended your faith but ended up being your pivot point? Scar. And listen, scars don't lie. They speak of surgeries that were necessary. They tell the truth that something had to be cut out so that life could continue. That's what healing looks like, not flawless skin, but closed wounds.

Scars Are Proof That Surgery Worked, Stop Hiding Them

Scars aren't shameful. They're sacred. But you'd never know that based on how most of us treat them. We live in a culture where we cover pain with polish, wrap trauma in trendy slogans, and call numbness "strength." We slap filters on our struggles and try to angle the camera of our lives just right, hoping no one sees the stitches underneath the smile. And yet, deep down, we all know this truth: healing always leaves a mark.

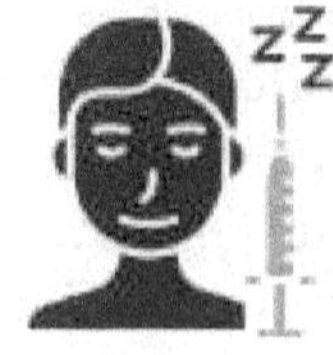

If you've walked with God for any length of time, and I mean really walked with Him, not just coasted on Sunday vibes or youth group highs, then you've likely experienced a form of divine surgery. The kind that cuts into your pride, slices through the illusion of control, exposes the hidden infection in your soul, and leaves you gutted, but finally healing. But here's the catch: most of us are terrified to show that kind of evidence. It's easier to pretend we never needed surgery. It's safer to just keep our wounds under wraps, hidden behind "I'm good, just tired," or "God's still working on me," while quietly bleeding inside. But Jesus didn't die for your image. He died for your soul.

Let's look again at **John 20:27 (NIV):** *"Then He said to Thomas, 'Put your finger here; see My hands. Reach out your hand and put it into My side. Stop doubting and believe.'"* Jesus didn't hide the very wounds that proved His resurrection. He *led* with them. He presented His scars not as signs of weakness, but as the ultimate proof of victory. Think about that. The Savior of the world chose to keep the scars. The Son of God, perfect, holy, eternal, resurrected with visible reminders of what He endured. Why? Because somebody needed to *see* it to believe it. Because somebody, maybe you, maybe your friend, maybe the kid sitting silent in the back row of your youth group, was waiting to see if wounds can really be healed.

Your scars are not your liability. They are your *credibility*. That anxiety attack you survived. It's a scar. That toxic relationship you escaped. It's a scar. That season of doubting God, feeling abandoned, drowning in depression, numbing out with substances, pushing everyone away, losing your sense of worth? That was your ICU. And you made it out. You might still be healing, but guess what? That means you're alive. You're in recovery. And in the Kingdom of God, *recovery is holy work.*

But healing, by nature, is uncomfortable. And the Church, let's be honest, hasn't always known what to do with discomfort. We've confused wholeness with polish. We've measured faith by performance. And we've accidentally taught people to only share their story *after* it's neatly wrapped in a bow, with all the lessons learned and no mess leaking out. We want testimonies, but we rush the surgery. We want healed people, but we don't make room for the healing process.

Here's the thing: scars don't show up until after the wound has closed. And wounds don't close until you've been *cut open*. That's why it's called surgery. God doesn't do surface work. He goes deep, deeper than your behavior, deeper than your image, deeper than what your friends know or your pastor suspects. He's not interested in spiritual performance. He wants transformation. And that kind of work leaves marks.

So, why do we keep hiding the scars? Fear. Shame. Pride. Maybe we're afraid that if people saw the real us, *the version that used to be hooked on approval, or pornography, or gossip, or self-harm, or bitterness*, they'd change their mind about our worth. Maybe we think that exposing the pain will reopen it. Maybe we've just gotten so good at performing, we've forgotten what it feels like to be honest. But the truth? Your scars are someone else's survival guide. When you stop hiding what God has healed, you give others permission to believe healing is possible for them too. That's not weakness. That's ministry. And before you say, "But I'm not ready to share yet," let me say this: there's wisdom in timing, but don't confuse that with silence rooted in shame. You don't have to be fully 'finished' to be useful. If you're two steps ahead of where you were, you've got something to share with someone still at the starting line. Healing doesn't require a platform. It requires *honesty*.

Look again at the woman with the issue of blood in **Luke 8:47**. She

was still bleeding when she reached out. Still messy. Still disqualified by society's standards. And yet, Jesus didn't shame her. He *highlighted* her. He allowed her healing to become a public moment, *on purpose*. Not to embarrass her, but to *elevate her faith*.

You don't have to wait until your story sounds neat to let it speak. And yes, some people will look at your scars and only see your past. They'll whisper about the old you. They'll doubt you're healing. That's okay. They're not the ones your testimony is for. Your story isn't meant to convince skeptics. It's meant to *rescue souls*. You don't need everyone's applause. You need someone's hope to be restored.

So, what if your scar makes church people uncomfortable? So, what if your past doesn't fit in with the small group icebreaker? This isn't about approval. It's about *freedom*. And freedom *always costs something*. This world is flooded with influences but starving for *authenticity*. We don't need more polished sermons and aesthetic quotes. We need believers who are willing to roll up their sleeves, point to the places where God cut, stitched, and healed, and say, "Here. This is where it happened. This is where He saved me from myself." That's the kind of testimony that shifts atmospheres. That's the kind of vulnerability that breaks cycles in families. That's the kind of honesty that awakens the next generation.

Because let's be real: Gen Z doesn't care about your suit or your sanctified language. They care about *truth*. About *real stories*. About the raw, unfiltered proof that God still does surgery and that people survive it. You are the proof.

So, if you're wondering whether to share your story, consider this your sign. Your scar isn't an accident. It's a calling. Let it speak. Let it point to the Surgeon. Let it testify to the fact that grace cuts deep but heals deeper. Let it remind the world that even when death tried to take you out, *Jesus got there first*, with a scalpel in hand and mercy on the table. And what He started in you? He's still finishing. So, show the scar. And let that be the loudest gospel you preach.

℞ Faith Clinic Reflection Page

Post-Op Notes: Healing in Review
Patient Name: ________________________________
Date of Reflection: ______________________________

Diagnostic Recap:

1. What are some of the "scars" in your life that you've tried to hide?

____

____

____

____

Write them down honestly. They might be emotional, spiritual, or relational.

2. How has God already begun healing some of those wounds? Describe the moments where you sensed breakthrough, peace, or closure, even if it was small.

____

____

____

____

3. Have you ever believed the lie that your scar disqualifies you? What made you think you had to cover up what God already covered with grace?

____

____

____

4. What's one way you can "show your scar" this week in a way that points to God's healing?

____

____

It could be through a conversation, a post, a testimony, or simply choosing not to hide anymore.

Soul Scan:

▨ I am in recovery, and I am proud of the progress. ▧ I still feel raw in some places, but I know God is working. ▨ I don't trust anyone with my wounds, and I'm afraid to show them. Circle one and ask: *What would it take for me to move closer to healing this week?*

Vital Signs Check:

- **Spiritual Honesty** → Am I being real with God about what still hurts?
- **Community Support** → Do I have people who know my scars and love me anyway?
- **Testimony Activation** → What story have I been too scared to share that someone else might need?

Prayer For Healing:

"God, the scars I carry are real, and some of them still sting. But I don't want to keep hiding what You've already healed. Help me trust that You can use my story, my past, my brokenness, and my restoration to bring life to others. Teach me how to show my scar with boldness, not to glorify the wound, but to glorify the One who stitched it back together. Amen."

📝 Faith Clinic Recovery Journal

Date: ______________________________

Journal Entry: ________________

🔍 **What Was Cut: What was the wound God began to heal in this season?** (*Describe what hurt, what broke, or what nearly took you out.*)

____

____

____

✂ **What Was Removed: What did God have to cut away?**
(*Pride, bitterness, fear, addiction, toxic relationships? Write it raw.*)

____

____

____

🧵 **Where the Surgeon Stitched: Where are you starting to see healing?** (*Are there areas where you feel lighter, more whole, or more honest?*)

____

____

____

✒ **The Scar That Remains: What story does your scar tell?**
(*Not your pain, but your progress. What have you learned?*)

"Me Too" Moments: Who needs to hear your story? (*Write the name or type of person who might find hope in your journey.*)

💬 My Bold Testimony Statement:

Complete this sentence:
"I'm not who I was, because God ________________________
(*Declare it as a truth over your life.*)

📖 Scripture Prescription for the Week:
(*Pick one to meditate on or memorize.*)

- **John 20:27** – *"Put your finger here; see My hands. Reach out your hand and put it into My side. Stop doubting and believe."*
- **Luke 8:47** – *"Then the woman, seeing that she could not go unnoticed, came trembling and fell at His feet..."*
- **Romans 8:1** – *"Therefore, there is now no condemnation for those who are in Christ Jesus."*

🕯 Prayer of Ownership:

"God, I admit I've been hiding parts of my story. Parts I've been ashamed of. But I see now that the scar is not a mark of shame, it's proof that You healed me. Give me boldness to live transparently. Use my story to help someone else. Let my scar speak of Your goodness, not my pain. Thank You for not leaving me in the middle of the operating room. You finished what You started. In Jesus' name, Amen."

PERSONAL NOTES

96

Chapter 4:

Spiritual Surgery, God Doesn't Use Anesthesia

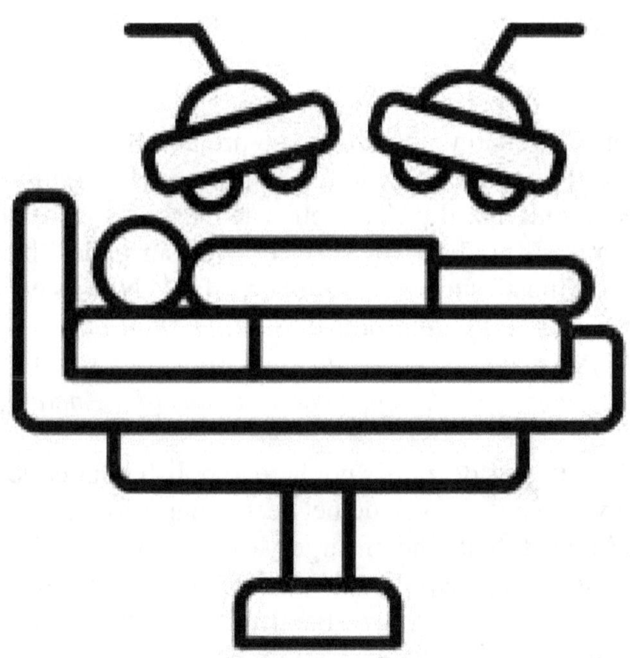

God's Scalpel: Precision Cuts In Places We Cover Up

There's a terrifying beauty in realizing that God doesn't do general surgery. He doesn't come in with a chainsaw and just start hacking away. No, our Creator, our Surgeon, uses a scalpel. A sharp, deliberate, holy tool. Precision over power. Accuracy over applause. He cuts exactly where it hurts, not because He wants to hurt us, but because He knows that hidden wounds are poisoning the rest of our spiritual bloodstream. And that's what makes it so uncomfortable.

Because let's be honest, we're good at covering things up. We layer on spiritual concealer: a perfect prayer life in public, a ministry title, a "God's got me" caption, even while we're bleeding privately under our Sunday best. We become experts in pretending not to limp when our soul has a compound fracture.

But God doesn't perform surgery through your filters. He doesn't operate on the version of you that you project, He goes after the real thing. The root of the infection. The bitterness behind your smile. Pride under your humility. The self-hate masked as confidence. And that requires surrender. Not surface-level surrender, but "cut me open if You must" surrender. **Hebrews 4:12 (NIV)** says: *"For the word of God is alive and active. Sharper than any double-edged sword, it penetrates even to dividing soul and spirit, joints and marrow; it judges the thoughts and attitudes of the heart."*

Notice that? It goes deep. It's not here to polish your edges, it's here to pierce your soul. To divide between what *looks* holy and what's healthy. And yes, that kind of surgery exposes things. It's not always your enemies being removed, sometimes it's your ego. Sometimes it's that coping mechanism you baptized as "God told me to distance myself." Sometimes it's your identity being rebuilt from the rubble of who you thought you had to be.

And when God places His finger on what we've buried, the pain we've spiritualized, the trauma we've turned into personality traits, it feels invasive. But hear this: sacred surgery feels like offense before it feels like freedom. Conviction will first make you flinch before it makes you whole. So, the next time you feel God pressing on something you didn't give Him access to, instead of running, lean in. That scalpel is love in motion.

There's something sobering about being spiritually dissected while fully awake. No anesthesia. No numbing agents. Just the clear and present awareness that God is cutting deep, and you can feel every inch of it. And the scariest part? You gave Him permission. Or at least, you thought you did when you prayed, "God, make me whole." We all want to be healed. But very few of us want it to be open. And fewer still are ready to deal with the mess that spills out once the scalpel hits the surface.

Here's the thing most of us don't talk about the areas we hide the best are usually the ones that hurt the most. And God, being who He is, doesn't start with the symptoms. He's not just interested in making your anxiety more manageable or your sin less obvious. He's not in the business of behavior modification; He's in the business of soul transformation. So, while you're asking Him to give you peace, He may be reaching instead for your need to control everything. While you're begging Him to take the depression, He might expose the identity crisis you've been ignoring for years. While you're asking Him to restore relationships, He may be cutting off the 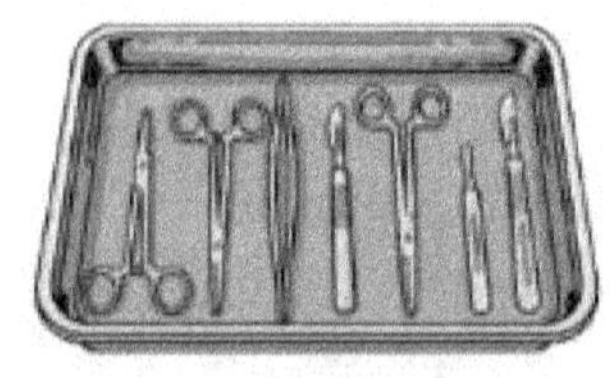 people you've used to medicate your emotional wounds. His goal is healing, but the path is often disrupted.

Ask any surgeon: real surgery is violent in its precision. It breaks skin, cuts through tissue, and exposes vulnerability. And once the opening starts, you can't stop midway and walk away. The worst thing to do during surgery is to move. And yet spiritually, so many of us flinch and run the moment we feel the first incision. We say things like, "God, I didn't sign up for all this." Or worse, "That's just how I am."

But here's the hard truth: spiritual growth demands that you stay on the table long enough for the healing to happen. That means not ghosting the process when it gets uncomfortable. That means resisting the urge to "church hop" every time a sermon feels personal. That means letting conviction linger, instead of burying it under distractions or busyness.

Let's be real, this generation is brilliant at distraction. We've mastered the art of numbing out. If you're hurting, just scroll. If you're anxious, binge something. If you're lonely, swipe. The problem is that distraction delays surgery. And delay always increases the risk of infection. What started as a wound from a breakup or a word curse from your childhood or a betrayal from a church leader can fester into bitterness, distrust, shame, or worse, a total spiritual shutdown. But when God, in His mercy, lays you bare on the table of transformation, He's not trying to embarrass you. He's trying to save your life. That's why His scalpel is so specific.

Ever noticed how God doesn't just "generally convict" you? He'll call out *that* text message. *That* lie you justified. *That* idol you renamed as ambition. He cuts with such clarity that it makes you feel exposed, and it should. Because exposure isn't the enemy; it's the invitation. Exposure is God's way of saying, "Let Me get to the thing that's been draining you in silence." **Psalm 139:23-24 (NIV)** says, "Search me, God, and know my heart; test me and know my anxious thoughts. See if there is any offensive way in me and lead me in the way everlasting."

Notice the request isn't, "Make me feel better," it's "Test me. Search for me. Lead me." That's surgical language. That's not a spiritual spa day, that's asking for open-heart correction. That's giving God permission to see all the parts you've carefully compartmentalized. And that's terrifying...until you realize who's holding the scalpel.

This isn't just some spiritual technician doing exploratory work. This is the Great Physician. The One who knit you together knows exactly where to cut and exactly how to close you up again. He doesn't cut to punish; He cuts to cure. But here's the kicker: you can't just ask for surgery and then fight the process when He lays you open. It doesn't work that way.

Healing will require you to face things you were comfortable forgetting. It will drag skeletons out of closets you thought were sealed. It will force you to grieve at things you tried to move past. But it will also give you the kind of freedom no shortcut can provide.

We often pray for God to use us. "Lord, use me for Your glory!" But do we really mean that? Because before God uses you publicly, He will always deal with you privately. And that private process feels personal. Like He's picking on you. Like He's putting your heart on blast while everyone else gets a pass. But don't confuse private surgery with punishment, it's preparation. God disciplines those He loves. (**Hebrews 12:6**). He corrects because He cares. His silence doesn't mean He's ignoring you. Sometimes, it means He's performing a deep work you wouldn't understand even if He explained it.

And here's where today's culture collides with God's method. We've been conditioned to expect quick fixes. One therapy session and the anxiety should disappear. One altar call and the trauma should dissolve. One journal entry and we should be good, right? But God is not in a rush. He doesn't treat symptoms; He goes after the source. And that means this surgery may take longer than you expected.

 You may find yourself cycling through layers of pain that you thought were handled years ago. But instead of getting discouraged, remember: the deeper the cut, the deeper the healing. You can't uproot years of dysfunction with a microwave prayer. You can't cleanse a soul infection with a five-minute devotion. The surgery is slow, but it's sacred.

And don't think for a second that God is grossed out by what He finds. That's another lie we tell ourselves. "If He sees this, He'll stop loving me." No, friend. He had already seen it. He's just waiting for you to hand Him the scalpel. He's waiting for you to stop rehearsing your shame and start revealing your wound. Because until you let Him touch it, He can't treat it. And untreated wounds don't disappear, they dictate. They shape your relationships, your beliefs, your behaviors, your boundaries. So, when God starts poking at something painful, don't assume it's judgment, it's surgery.

Let me tell you something raw: the only thing more painful than letting God cut it out...is trying to live with it still in you. So, what does this mean for today? How do you live this out practically?

1. **Stay on the table**, When you feel God confronting an area, resist the urge to distract, numb, or run. Stay present with it. Stay in the discomfort long enough to hear what He's after.
2. **Stop self-diagnosing**, Just because you think it's "not that bad" doesn't mean it's not lethal. Let the Word examine you. Let the Spirit convict you. Let mature believers speak truth even if it stings.
3. **Invite inspection**, Ask God daily, "Where do You want to cut today?" Invite the Holy Spirit to probe, press, and

pinpoint. You don't need a performance. You need a procedure.

4. **Let others testify**, Surround yourself with people who've survived surgery. Not the ones still covering up their wounds, but the ones who say, "Let me show you where He opened me up, and what He removed."

5. **Trust the Healer**, Remember, He's not cutting to harm you. He's cutting to make you whole. And when you heal, you'll carry not just a scar, but a story that can save someone else.

So, if it's hurting right now, good. That means the scalpel is working. That means the infection is being removed. That means the lie is being exposed. That means the heart of stone is becoming fresh again. That means healing is happening...even if you can't see it yet. And one day, when the scar has formed and the strength has returned, you'll be able to look someone else in the eye and say: "I've been there. I know that pain. But He cut it out, and I lived."

You'll realize that the places you bless the most are now the places you bless the most. You'll stop resenting the surgery. And you'll start worshipping the Surgeon.

What Spiritual Surgery Looks Like
(Hint: Vulnerability, Not Vibes)

We live in a world addicted to appearances. Where "healing" often gets reduced to an aesthetic, where you post a glowing Instagram reel of a worship night, caption it with "God is good," and call that spiritual breakthrough. But true spiritual surgery? It doesn't fit in a highlight reel. It doesn't come with a cute filter. It doesn't always feel good, sound good, or look good. And it doesn't go viral. Because real healing, healing that changes the trajectory of your life, looks like vulnerability, not vibes.

Spiritual surgery is when God reaches into the places you pretend don't exist. The bitterness you baptize in busyness. The unforgiveness you dress up with service. The pain you numb with overcommitment, or worse, over-spiritualization. It's not always a dramatic altar call or a mountain-top epiphany.

 Sometimes it's sitting in your car, crying because you finally admitted that you're exhausted from pretending to be okay. Sometimes it's canceling plans because you're finally prioritizing your mental health over people-pleasing. Sometimes it's the moment you stop quoting scriptures to avoid your emotions and start letting God dissect the ones behind your silence.

God doesn't go for the surface. He doesn't waste time fixing the makeup of your faith when the muscle is infected. When He does surgery, He goes deep. **Hebrews 4:12 (NIV)** says it clearly: *"For the word of God is alive and active. Sharper than any double-edged sword, it penetrates even to dividing soul and spirit, joints and marrow; it judges the thoughts and attitudes of the heart."* That's what God does. He divides what you do from who you are. He separates how you worship from why you worship. And then, He starts cutting.

The operating table isn't glamorous. It looks like prayer that sounds more like groaning. It looks like accountability that stings. It looks like showing up for your friends even when your anxiety is trying to isolate you. It looks like journaling about the father wound you keep dodging or the identity issue you spiritualized as "just being humble." It looks like reading scripture not to post it but to apply it. It looks like admitting that healing is inconvenient, uncomfortable, and deeply necessary.

You want to know what spiritual surgery sounds like? It's the sigh you let out after being honest in therapy for the first time. It's the awkward silence after you admit in group that you don't trust God with your finances. It's the gut-punch conviction when a sermon hits too close to home and you're mad because it exposed what you swore you buried. That's the scalpel in action.

And here's the thing about surgery: you can't perform it on yourself. You need to submit. You need to be still. You need to let the Holy Spirit do what only He can do, because when you try to heal yourself, you'll stitch up wounds with pride, shame, hustle, or avoidance. And those aren't healing tools. Those are infection traps. Vulnerability means laying there and saying, "God, cut what You need to cut." It's letting go of what you thought healing should look like. It's dropping your defense mechanisms and finally letting God tear down the idols you've made from ministry, relationships, or even your own trauma. It's ugly. But it's real. And real is where God works best.

 If you're going through spiritual surgery right now, this is your confirmation: the pain you're feeling isn't punishment, it's precision. God is not trying to destroy you. He's trying to save what's still worth salvaging. He's removing what's killing you softly, your people-pleasing, your comparison, your toxic self-talk, your hustle to earn what's already yours by grace.

So, the next time you feel exposed, cracked open, raw with conviction, and unsure of how you'll put yourself back together, don't run. That's the scalpel. That's the cut. That's the start of something sacred. It's the beginning of being made whole.

You can't fast-track spiritual surgery. There's no drive-thru deliverance, no five-step YouTube tutorial that teaches you how to be emotionally whole. Real healing doesn't come with a deadline; it comes with discomfort. And that's the part nobody puts in the revival promo. They'll sell you miracles, but they won't tell you that the healing might first feel like heartbreak. That the peace you're praying for might come only after God disrupts the patterns you've grown addicted to.

You want to know what God's surgical table really feels like? It feels like your entire life stops making sense. The prayers don't hit the same. The worship songs that used to move you now feel distant. Your old coping mechanisms aren't numb like they used to. And your faith, which once felt like armor, suddenly starts to feel like an exposed nerve. You're not crazy. You're not broken beyond repair. You're in surgery. And surgery isn't soft. It's sharp. It slices before it stitches.

Some of the deepest work God does in us is not through blessings but through breaking. Not through applause but through silence. Not through convenience but through cutting. Because contrary to popular church clichés, God's priority isn't your comfort, it's your character. And the character He's forming in you can't be built in atmospheres that only favor performance. It's built in raw, holy, unfiltered places where your soul is cracked wide open and you have no choice but to finally let Him touch what you've kept hidden.

Let's get personal. Think about the thing you don't want anyone to bring up, the insecurity, the failure, the secret you've spiritualized into silence. That's probably the place God is trying to heal. But healing it means you must stop defending it. It means you must stop hiding it under "I'm good" responses and fake laughter. It means telling the truth, even when it hurts. That's not weakness. That's vulnerability. And vulnerability is the scalpel that opens the heart to transformation.

And no, vibes don't cut deep enough. You can "feel God" and still not let Him change you. You can jump during worship and still limp through Monday, emotionally dehydrated and spiritually distant. Because goosebumps don't equal growth. You've got to move past the aesthetic of faith and into the anatomy of faith, the part where God rearranges the way you think, love, trust, forgive, and function. The part that hurts, then heals.

It's in that place that the real testimonies begin. One young man I worked with put it like this: "I didn't realize I was using church to hide from God. I thought showing up was enough. But then I started therapy, and it was like God turned the lights on in every room I'd locked shut. I cried more in six weeks than I had in six years. But for the first time, I felt clean. Not perfect. Just clean. Like something infected had finally been removed." That's spiritual surgery. It's the messy confession at 2 a.m. when you tell your best friend you've been silently battling depression while posting "God is good" graphics.

It's the moment you finally delete the contact that's been pulling 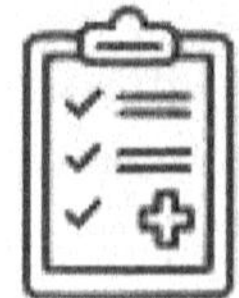 you back into toxic cycles you call "just hanging out." It's when you stop excusing your trust issues with "that's just how I am," and admit, "I actually need help learning how to be loved again." It's vulnerable. It's not aesthetic. And it's holy.

The problem is that vulnerability feels like weakness to a culture trained to curate perfection. We hide the process because we want to protect our image. But God can't heal what you pretend isn't hurt. You must be willing to unravel. And when you finally stop managing your appearance and start surrendering your actual heart, He begins to perform a kind of internal surgery no worship set or motivational quote could ever replicate.

So yes, it might look like you breaking down in the car on your lunch break. It might look like calling your mom and apologizing for the years of resentment. It might look like writing the letter to your younger self that says, "You didn't deserve what happened, but healing is your birthright now." These are not vibes. These are victories. These are the scars of surgery that saved your life. And the most powerful part? You don't go through it alone.

Psalm 34:18 (NIV) reminds us, *"The Lord is close to the brokenhearted and saves those who are crushed in spirit."* He's not repelled by your brokenness. He's not turned off by your honesty. In fact, that's where He does His best work, when you finally lay yourself bare and say, "Cut what needs to be cut, God. I trust You to heal me."

This generation doesn't need more polished faith. It needs bold, surgical-level surrender. The kind that costs you your pride but gains you your peace. The kind that doesn't wait for Sunday service to change but let's God start the transformation on a random Tuesday afternoon. That's where the healing lives, in the hidden places where vibes can't reach, but vulnerability invites God in.

So, here's the challenge: Will you stop vibing your way through brokenness and let God do what He came to do? Because healing doesn't come through aesthetics. It comes through surgery. And God is ready to operate.

Testimonies From Youth Who Felt "Ripped Open" Before Breakthrough

They didn't teach us this part in youth group. Nobody passed out flyers that said, *"Welcome to the wilderness, please fasten your seatbelt and prepare for emotional turbulence."* No, we got memory verses, pizza parties, and just enough worship lyrics to feel holy on a Sunday. But when the pain came,  when life hit like a freight train, none of that felt like enough. What nobody told us is that real breakthroughs often come wrapped in real breakthroughs.

Let's start with Camila. She's 17, quiet, artistic, and had mastered the role of the "good church girl." She served on the youth worship team, knew every lyric to every Elevation Worship song, and never missed a Sunday. But behind her worship  smile was a deep, soul-level exhaustion. "I didn't realize I was spiritually empty until I started crying during rehearsal," she said. "It wasn't because the song moved me, it was because I couldn't take it anymore. I felt like I was performing for God instead of worshiping Him."

That breakdown led to a breakthrough. Camila began seeing a counselor her church recommended. She started journaling prayers that sounded more like desperate confessions than polished petitions. And somewhere in the middle of that unraveling, she met the Jesus who doesn't need performances, just permission. "God didn't show up when I got louder," she said. "He showed up when I got honest."

Then there's Elijah, 19, who came into the Faith Clinic program thinking it would be a cute summer Bible study. What he didn't expect was to be confronted with the truth about his addiction to approval. "I thought I was just being social," Elijah explained, "but really, I couldn't go five minutes without checking if someone liked my post, my outfit, my vibe. I didn't realize I was worshiping attention."

Elijah's turning point came during a week-long fast. "I had to sit in silence with no distractions. That's when I realized I was lonely. Not just 'need a friend's loneliness but soul-level, I-don't-even-know-myself lonely. And I couldn't fill it with noise anymore." The silence became surgery. God cut through the layers of performative joy and got to the root: fear of rejection. That's when healing finally started. Now, Elijah leads small group sessions about identity. Not because he's perfect, but because he remembers what it's like to not know who you are.

Zariah, 16, shared her story at the Faith Clinic retreat. "I thought my depression made me spiritually broken," she said. "Like I was failing God because I couldn't be happy." But after attending a session on mental wellness and faith, she began to understand that spiritual sickness doesn't disqualify you from spiritual healing. "My breakthrough didn't come when I stopped crying," she said. "It came when I let someone pray with me while I was still crying."

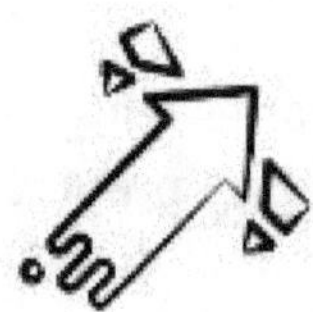 These testimonies aren't tidy. They're not always wrapped in perfect endings or tied with a scripture bow. But they're real. And they all echo one central truth: before God rebuilds you, He will often allow you to be unmade. Not because He enjoys your pain, but because He knows healing doesn't happen on the surface. It happens in the parts of you that you've hidden even from yourself. That's the surgery. It's the moment when a teenager realizes that cutting off toxic friendships feels worse than staying but staying is killing their purpose. It's the night when a student leader finally admits that they've been scrolling for validation instead of opening their Bible. It's the morning after a panic attack when a youth pastor says, "You're still loved, even when you're not okay."

Romans 5:3-4 (NIV) say this: *"Not only so, but we also glory in our sufferings, because we know that suffering produces perseverance; perseverance, character; and character, hope."*

Pain, perseverance, character, hope. That's the surgical path. It's not inspirational, it's invasive. But that's the gospel at work in real lives. Not Insta-worthy. Not filtered. Just honest.

In every one of these testimonies, one thing is clear: God does not abandon you on the operating table. He stays. He holds. He weeps with you. He cuts carefully, not cruelly. And when you finally rise, bruised, stitched up, but stronger, you'll carry a testimony that doesn't just tell people God is good; it *proves* it. That's what breakthrough looks like. It's not always loud. It's often painful. But it's always holy.

Testimonies From Youth Who Felt
"Ripped Open" Before Breakthrough

They didn't expect their first real encounter with God to feel more like emergency surgery than a warm hug. For most of the teens and young adults walking through their first season of conviction and transformation, the shock wasn't in the sin being exposed, it was in how deeply it had taken root.

One young woman, 17-year-old Leah, shared how her anxiety attacks weren't just emotional meltdowns but symptoms of a deeper spiritual infection: performance-based faith. "I thought if I did everything right, youth group, worship team, straight A's, that God would give me peace," she said. "But I was exhausted. It wasn't until everything broke down that I realized I never trusted Him, I just feared disappointing Him." Her moment of breakthrough came not in a fire tunnel or at a conference, but on her bedroom floor when she cried out, "God, if You're real, show me who I really am without all the noise." The peace didn't come immediately. What came first was silence, followed by truth that wrecked her pride. Then came healing.

Malik, a 19-year-old college freshman, had built his life on achievements and approval. He was the first in his family to go to college, carried the weight of everyone's expectations, and learned to numb his fear of failure with distractions, parties, people-pleasing, and overcommitting. "God wasn't a Father to me," he said. "He was a scoreboard." The surgery hit when he failed two classes and had to withdraw. "I felt worthless. I felt like my identity was a GPA." It wasn't a sermon or retreat that reached him. It was a campus ministry leader who looked him in the eye and said, "You're not broken because you failed. You're being broken so you can heal from thinking your worth was in your wins." That was the scalpel, truth that sliced through his false identity. Malik said the healing started when he stopped pretending, he was fine and asked God to rebuild what was underneath the image. "It hurt. Like, I had to mourn the version of myself I created. But I've never felt more like myself than I do now."

These aren't dramatic testimonies designed to entertain; they're everyday spiritual surgeries that so many youths are walking through quietly. The pain of being "ripped open" isn't always external. Sometimes it's the breakdown of internal beliefs. The kind of beliefs that say, "I'm only lovable if I perform," or "I have to fix myself before I come to God." One high schooler, Isaiah, shared that his breakthrough came during a discipleship small group, not in the middle of deep worship or a revival service. "They asked one question: 'What's one lie you believe about yourself that God didn't say?' I broke. I didn't even realize I believed I was disposable until someone gave me permission to confront it."

The themes in these stories aren't isolated. They're consistent. Most youth don't need another hype moment; they need healing encounters. And those often begin with painful awareness. One young woman described her encounter like this: "It felt like God ripped the band aid off every place I was trying to cover. At first, I wanted to run. But then I realized, He wasn't trying to shame me. He was exposing it so He could treat it." Another student said, "It was like God held a mirror to my heart. And I hated what I saw. But He stayed in the room with me. He didn't flinch."

That's what spiritual surgery looks like for this generation, deep, raw, honest, and very often unexpected. It's not about theatrics. It's about encounters. One youth pastor put it this way: "They're not walking out because they hate God. They're walking out because no one ever gave them space to bleed honestly. The church must shift from image-management to soul-care. Because real healing starts where the pain is, and sometimes that means cutting through years of spiritual numbing agents: religious performance, suppressed trauma, masked depression, and buried questions.

As we prepare to move to the final section of this chapter, let this be the message we pass down to every young person: Feeling "ripped open" isn't a sign that something went wrong. It's a sign that God's hands are on you, doing what only a Great Physician can do. And the only thing more painful than that kind of surgery... is avoiding it.

The Pain That Leads To Purpose

It's easy to quote **Romans 8:28** when everything's fine, when the bills are paid, the mental health is manageable, and you're not crying into your pillow every night wondering if God still sees you. But when life cuts deep, when the job is lost, the betrayal hits, or the depression lingers longer than your devotional streak, the idea that "all things work together for good" can feel more like a cruel joke than a comforting promise.

Yet here's the unfiltered truth: purpose is almost always birthed through pain. Not convenient. No applause. Not spiritual vibes. Pain. We don't like this reality. In fact, most of us spend our lives trying to avoid pain. We pray for it away, numb it with distractions, over-spiritualize our denial, or fake smiles to mask the internal bruises. But the Kingdom of God operates on a completely different prescription plan. Pain isn't just permitted; it's often the catalyst for your calling.

Take Joseph, for example. God gave him a dream but didn't fast-track him to the palace. He went through betrayal, abandonment, false accusations, prison, basically the worst group project ever. His purpose to save nations didn't emerge on the mountaintop. It was developed in the pit, in the prison, in the places where his character was chiseled and his faith refined. His pain didn't delay his purpose; it *produced* it.

Purpose isn't microwaveable. You don't get to skip suffering and still expect to walk in anointing that breaks chains. You can't lead others out of bond if you've never learned to bleed and still believe. Real ministry, real purpose, real impact all comes at a cost. And that cost is usually a season that feels like a surgical table, where God begins cutting away everything that can't go with you to the next level.

Some of your greatest assignments will come from your most painful experiences. The girl who survived sexual abuse and now walks with other survivors. The guy who lost his father and now mentors young boys growing up without one. The teen who battled suicidal thoughts and now shares her story so others know they're not alone. They didn't just *live through* something hard they let God *lead through* it.

Here's where it gets gritty: pain is not proof that God has abandoned you. In fact, it might be the loudest indicator that He's working on something eternal in you. **2 Corinthians 4:17 (NIV)** says, "For our light and momentary troubles are achieving for us an eternal glory that far outweighs them all." Notice the word: *achieving*. Your trouble is working. It's not wasted. It's achieving something. But you must stay at the table. That's the hardest part. Most of us want to escape before the surgery is over. We want healing without surrender, purpose without pruning. But if you jump off the table too early, if you abandon the process, then the wound remains, the infection spreads, and the pain never transforms into power.

Ask any surgeon: the most delicate, vital work happens once the surface has been opened. God's not trying to embarrass you. He's trying to restore you. He's going beneath the surface, beneath the performance, the insecurity, the shame, the addiction, and He's exposing what's infected so He can breathe new life into it.

The pain isn't punishment. It's preparation. **Isaiah 61:3** says He gives "beauty for ashes, the oil of joy for mourning, the garment of praise for the spirit of despair." But He can't exchange what you refuse to admit you're holding. You must hand Him the ashes. You must let Him see the mourning. That takes honesty. Vulnerability. And yes, pain.

But on the other side of that is purpose so pure it'll bring tears to your eyes. Not because it's perfect, but because it's finally *real*.

That's the faith clinic prescription: let the pain do its work. Don't numb it. Don't escape it. Don't pretend you're fine. Let God cut deep, so He can heal wide. Let Him remove what you've outgrown. Let Him confront what's been killing your soul slowly. It will hurt, but it will also transform.

And when you come out on the other side, scarred but standing, you'll be able to say: "This pain had a purpose. This wasn't just suffering, it was sanctification. It wasn't just hard, it was holy." And your story? It'll no longer be about what broke you. It'll be about what you built.

🩺 Faith Clinic Patient File: Post-Op Reflection

Name: _______________________________
Date of Surgery (Reading): _______________________

Spiritual Vital Signs Check:

- 🔍 Honesty Level: ☐ Numb ☐ Anxious ☐ Raw ☐ Vulnerable ☐ Healing
- 💬 Prayer Activity: ☐ Avoidant ☐ Surface Level ☐ Broken and Honest
- 🖤 Heart Exposure Level: ☐ Hidden ☐ Slightly Open ☐ Fully on the Table

🔍 **Diagnostic Questions (Write Your Answers Honestly)**

1. **What area of your life has God been trying to "cut into" but you've been numbing or avoiding it?** *Be honest. What have you been covering up because it feels too painful or too messy to address?*

____

____

____

2. **Describe a moment when your soul felt like it was in "surgery." What did God remove or reveal?** *Was it pride, bitterness, fear, an addiction, or something you thought you needed to survive?*

____

____

____

3. How have you viewed pain in the past, punishment or process? What changed after reading this chapter?

____

____

____

4. Do you believe that God can use your pain for purpose? What part of your story could become someone else's survival guide?

____

____

____

♥ Faith Rx Prescription Pad

Spiritual Dosage:

☐ Read Isaiah 61:1–4 daily this week

☐ Write a letter to your "old self", the one that was bleeding, broken, or lost

☐ Identify 1 scar (emotional, relational, spiritual) and journal how God used it to heal you

Next Check-Up Reminder: "God doesn't heal what we hide. He heals what we hand Him."

✍ Journal Prompt:

Write about one painful season of your life where God allowed you to be "cut open" spiritually, and what came out of it. What did He remove? What did He stitch back together? What do you now carry differently because of that procedure?

Use this space to pour it all out. No filter. No edits. Just raw reflection.

📖 Scripture Refills To Meditate On:

- **Psalm 147:3 (NIV)** – *"He heals the brokenhearted and binds up their wounds."*
- **Hebrews 12:11 (NIV)** – *"No discipline seems pleasant at the time, but painful. Later, however, it produces a harvest of righteousness and peace..."*
- **Romans 8:18 (NIV)** – *"I consider that our present sufferings are not worth comparing with the glory that will be revealed in us."*

Reflections

____

____

____

____

____

____

____

____

____

Chapter 5:

Stop Asking For Healing When You Won't Change Your Diet

⚕ *You're Not Hungry, You're Addicted*

Let's tell the truth: some of us aren't sick, we're spiritually malnourished, and it's not because God isn't feeding us. It's because we keep reaching for junk. And just like someone in the ER with chest pains but refuses to let go of the fried food that clogged their arteries, we show up in God's presence asking for healing but keep going back to the same toxic diet that broke us in the first place.

Imagine showing up to the emergency room with stomach pain, and when the doctor says it's food poisoning, you ask him to fix you, *without* giving up the rotten food you're still eating. That's how we treat God. We ask for supernatural healing but hold on to soul habits that poisoned us to begin with. We want relief, not change. We want healing, not discipline. We want resurrection without crucifixion. And then we wonder why we keep getting spiritually sick again.

This chapter is your prescription for long-term healing. Not just band-aids. Not just goosebump Sundays. But the lifestyle shifts that keep the healing *you already received*. Because let's be real, it's not that God didn't move the last time. It's that you kept feeding the disease He delivered you from.

The Role Of Obedience In Staying Healed

Let's be blunt: obedience is not just God's suggestion, it's your aftercare. It's the "take these meds exactly as prescribed" note after your spiritual surgery. But most of us ignore the label. We skip doses. We throw away instructions. Then we cry when we relapse. In **John 5:14**, Jesus heals a man at the pool of Bethesda, but after the healing, He says something jarring: "See, you are well again. Stop sinning or something worse may happen to you."

Now hold up. You mean Jesus just healed this man and then dropped that kind of warning? Yup. Because healing isn't just about the miracle. It's about maintenance. It's about a lifestyle that aligns with the wholeness God just gave you. Jesus wasn't being harsh; He was being honest. Some of us don't need *another* touch. We need to honor the one we already have.

Obedience is often treated like a chore. But biblically, it's medicine. Obedience doesn't just protect your healing, it multiplies it. It creates space in your life for God's Word to take root and bear fruit. The issue is, we like inspiration more than instruction. We love worship but avoid the Word. We want prophecy but ignore practice. Youth today are facing more distractions and options than ever before, and obedience isn't flashy. But let's talk practically: if God healed you from anxiety, obedience might look like setting boundaries with toxic people. If He restored your identity, obedience might mean deleting apps that feed your comparison addiction.

Obedience is specific. Personal. And often inconvenient. That's why it's powerful. Because it goes *against* what your flesh wants to do, and that's what makes room for your spirit to grow. Obedience doesn't earn healing, but it honors it. It tells God, "What You did in me matters enough for me to shift everything." So, here's a sobering truth: your miracle is God's mercy, but your lifestyle is your stewardship. Healing isn't a moment. It's a movement. It doesn't stop at the altar, it continues in your choices. Obedience is not about perfection; it's about positioning yourself to *keep* what God gave you.

Ask yourself: What did God already heal you from, and what habits did you run back to? What part of your diet still contradicts your delivery? Because sometimes the greatest evidence of faith isn't what you say in worship, it's what you refuse to feed once you walk out the church doors. It's easy to cry out to God in desperation. Pain makes us open. Suffering makes us surrender. And in the middle of our mess, we say things like, "God, I'll do *anything* if You just fix this." But what happens after the pain lifts? After the altar call ends. After the anxiety calms, the relationship is restored, the peace returns, and the spiritual high fades into Monday morning real life.

 That's where obedience comes in. Not the emotional, momentary surrender, but the daily, inconvenient kind. The kind that says "yes" to God when nobody's looking. The kind that deletes the contact, blocks the number, shows up to church tired, opens your Bible even when you feel nothing, and honors the boundaries God gave you *after* He healed you.

Obedience is how you protect what God has done. It's the after-surgery recovery plan, the post-op instructions for your soul. It's saying, "I don't just want to *feel* better, I want to *live* better." But let's be honest. Obedience isn't cute. It doesn't come with claps or comments. It doesn't trend on social media. It's not always exciting or emotionally fulfilling. Sometimes it feels like restriction. Like loss. Like saying no when you're used to saying yes. Like walking away from the "almost" that almost made you forget your worth. Like choosing worship when you'd rather scroll. Like confronting yourself when nobody else will. And yet, it's the very thing that keeps you healed. Remember the ten lepers in Luke 17? All ten cried out for healing. All ten received it. But only one came back. Only one returned to thank Jesus. Only one recognized that the healing wasn't the end, it was the beginning. And what did Jesus say to him? "Rise and go; your faith have made you well." (**Luke 17:19 NIV**)

The others were healed *externally*. But only the one who returned in obedience was healed *completely*. There's something about obeying after the miracle that opens the door for a deeper kind of wellness.

In our culture, we often equate healing with a feeling, "I feel free now," "I feel strong again," "I feel like I've moved on." But feelings fade. Emotions shift. And if your healing is rooted in emotion instead of obedience, you'll find yourself circling the same issues, revisiting the same pain, praying for deliverance from cycles you keep feeding with disobedience.

Let's talk plainly: obedience may mean ending that relationship God already told you to leave. It may mean forgiving the person you swore you never would. It may mean humbling yourself and going to therapy. It may mean leaving the environment that feeds your addiction. It may mean confronting the parts of your identity that are built more on pain than on God's promises.

Obedience is God's way of preserving what He restored. Think of it like this, if God healed your heart but you keep texting your trauma, it's not that He didn't do His part. It's that you reopened the wound with your choices. Healing is not just about divine intervention; it's about *human agreement*. It's saying with your *life* what you once said with your *lips*: "God, I trust You more than I trust my feelings."

This generation is often told that grace covers everything, and that's true. But grace doesn't cancel obedience. Grace empowers it. Grace is not permission to stay sick. It's strength to walk in freedom. As Paul says in **Romans 6:1-2 (NIV):** "Shall we go on sinning so that grace may increase? By no means! We are those who have died to sin; how can we live in it any longer?"

Healing requires partnership. God is the Surgeon, yes. But you're the patient who must choose to follow the prescription. That means changing your schedule, your input, your relationships, your priorities. That means aligning your life with the healing you prayed for.

A healed soul that won't obey God is like a bandaged wound that never gets air. You suffocate what God's trying to grow. You clog what He's trying to clear. You stay sick, not because God didn't move, but because you won't move with Him. And let's be real, obedience is hard because it costs you. It costs comfort. It costs pride. It costs old identities and habits. But it also leads to *fruit*. It leads to peace, wholeness, growth, and lasting change. So, here's the question: What has God already healed that you're risking with your current diet?

Obedience doesn't make God love you more. But it does position you to experience the *fullness* of His love. Not just in moments, but in movements. In lifestyles. In daily disciplines that say, "I'm not going back to who I was before God touched me." Obedience is how you honor the healing. Obedience is how you protect progress. Obedience is the medicine that keeps the soul aligned.

So, if you've been crying out for healing while ignoring God's instructions, maybe it's time to stop praying for a miracle and start walking in obedience. Because He already healed you. He already set you free. Now the ball is in your court. Will you keep the change? Will you protect the breakthrough? Will you change your diet? Or will you keep asking God to fix what your habits continue to break?

Spiritual Junk Food Blocks Your Growth

Bitterness. Distraction. People-Pleasing.

You wouldn't eat candy for breakfast, soda for lunch, or cookies for dinner, then complain about feeling sluggish and sick. But that's exactly what we do spiritually. We're snacking on bitterness,

chewing on old offenses, rerunning mental highlight reels of who hurt us. That's spiritual acid reflux. Bitterness poisons the soul from the inside out. **Hebrews 12:15** warns: *"See to it that no bitter root grows up to cause trouble and defile many."*

Bitterness doesn't stay small. It takes root. It spreads. It leaks into your friendships, your worship, even your theology. You start blaming God for wounds people inflicted. You can't grow with that kind of toxicity. That's junk food. That's processed trauma. Distraction is another favorite meal of the enemy. The enemy doesn't always need to destroy you; he just needs to keep you distracted long enough to delay your destiny. TikTok binges, scrolling for hours, comparing your life to someone else's highlight reel… it adds up. It numbs you. It fills you with noise until there's no room left to hear God.

And let's talk about people-pleasing. That's a whole buffet of spiritual malnutrition. You keep feeding your need to be liked, validated, needed. You say "yes" when God told you to say "no." You perform when He asked you to rest. You overcommit and call it service when it's really a search for worth. That diet leads to burning out. Fast.

Paul didn't mince words in **Galatians 1:10**, *"Am I now trying to win the approval of human beings, or of God? If I were still trying to please people, I would not be a servant of Christ."*

Let that sink in.

If your diet is fueled by the applause of others, you'll never be nourished by the presence of God. So, what's your diet today? Are you feeding on validation instead of the Word? Are you snacking on gossip and calling it "processing"? Are you feeding old wounds more than your faith?

Spiritual junk food feels good going down, but it stunts your growth. You stay bloated with comparison. You stay tired from offense. You stay stuck in loops that God already gave you power to break. It's time to clean out your pantry. No more soul-snacks that keep you sick. No more emotional carbs that make you crash. You don't need another inspirational quote; you need a diet plan. One that includes *truth*, not just *comfort*.

We all know what junk food does to the body. It's quick. It's satisfying for the moment. It's everywhere, convenient and cheap. But over time, it leaves your body sluggish, your mind foggy, and your system bloated with stuff it was never meant to digest. Now, apply that same concept to your soul. What you feed your spirit determines your strength, and many of us are spiritually malnourished not because God isn't showing up, but because we keep reaching for spiritual Doritos when we need divine nutrition.

Let's call it what it is: bitterness, distractions, people-pleasing, codependency, toxic scrolling, constant comparison, gossip, busyness dressed up as purpose, all of it, spiritual junk food. It tasted good for a minute. It gives the illusion of being full. But it's empty. Hollow. Non-nutritious. And worst of all, it slowly kills your appetite for the things that *feed you*.

One of the most dangerous symptoms of a spiritual junk food diet is numbness, the inability to recognize you're not well. You don't feel conviction anymore. You can't hear God clearly. You're too full of noise to recognize the silence. You start calling apathy "peace," and you mistake distraction for rest. You think you're doing okay because you're still busy, but busy doesn't mean fed. Busy doesn't mean aligned. Busy doesn't mean obedient.

Let's talk about *bitterness* for a moment. Bitterness is one of the most common forms of soul junk food because it's often justified. You were hurt. They did betray you. It wasn't fair. But bitterness tricks you into thinking you're strong because you're guarded. It hardens your heart to the point where even God's voice can't get through the layers.

Hebrews 12:15 (NIV) says, *"See to it that no one falls short of the grace of God and that no bitter root grows up to cause trouble and defile many."*

Notice that it doesn't just say *you* will be troubled. It says bitterness *defiles many*. It spreads. It becomes a toxin that leeches into your relationships, your thoughts, your choices. You cannot grow spiritually while feasting on bitterness. Forgiveness is the detox, and obedience is the new diet.

What about *distraction*? We live in a world of constant stimulation. If we're not scrolling, we're binge-watching. If we're not texting, we switch between apps. We consume more content in a day than generations before us did in a year. And yet we wonder why we can't hear God. Why do we feel dry. Why is nothing changing. Distraction is one of the devil's most successful weapons, not because it's evil, but because it's *effective*. It doesn't need to be sinful to be a weapon. It just needs to be consistent enough to numb you.

Then there's *people-pleasing*. At first, it feels noble. It feels Christlike. You're putting others first, you're being generous, you're not starting conflict. But when your peace depends on someone else's opinion, you're not pleasing people, you're being ruled by them.

Galatians 1:10 (NIV) asks the hard question: *"Am I now trying to win the approval of human beings, or of God? ... If I were still trying to please people, I would not be a servant of Christ."* Spiritual junk food isn't always obvious. Sometimes it's labeled as love. Sometimes it hides under the disguise of loyalty. Sometimes it wears church clothes and talks like wisdom. But if it leaves you drained, disconnected, distracted, or disobedient, it's junk. Period.

Let's take a moment to reflect on how Jesus approached spiritual nutrition. In Matthew 4, after forty days of fasting, Satan comes to tempt Jesus with the immediate, "Turn these stones to bread." That was junk food. Not because bread is bad, but because it was a shortcut. An easy fill for a deep hunger. But Jesus responds, "Man shall not live on bread alone, but on every word that comes from the mouth of God." **(Matthew 4:4 NIV)**

Have you heard of that? *Every word.* Not just the highlight reel. Not just the feel-good verses. Not just the prosperity promises. But every word, even the hard ones. Even the parts that confront you. Even the truth that makes you uncomfortable. That's a full meal. That's whole-food spirituality. That's the diet of a disciple. So how do you know if you're living off spiritual junk food?

Here's a quick soul check:

- Are you more informed by reels than the Word?
- Do you spend more time managing your brand than managing your heart?
- Are your prayers mostly about others changing, and not about God changing you?
- Do you feel empty after being around certain people, shows, or platforms, but you keep returning anyway?
- Do you feed your emotions more than your spirit?

If the answer is yes to any of the above, don't panic. But don't ignore it either. Just like a physical diet requires intentional change, so does a spiritual one. You can't fast from distraction for a day and expect a miracle. You need consistency. You need a new rhythm. You need soul nutrition that lasts longer than a sermon clip.

Psalm 34:8 (NIV) says, "Taste and see that the Lord is good; blessed is the one who takes refuge in Him." There's an invitation in that verse, not to just *hear* God's Word, but to *taste* it. To chew on it. To digest it. To let it become part of you. Junk food slides down easily. Real food takes time. Effort. Preparation. But it nourishes you in ways junk never can.

And let's not forget just like with physical junk food, the more you consume, the more you crave it. But the reverse is also true. The more you feed your spirit with real nourishment, prayer, Scripture, community, silence, obedience, the more your appetite shifts. What once satisfied you won't anymore. The gossip won't hit the same. The late-night scrolling won't do it. The attention you used to crave will feel small compared to the presence of God.

So, here's your reality check: you can't keep crying out for healing if your diet is poisoning your progress. Stop praying for breakthrough while binging on bitterness. Stop asking for peace while feeding chaos. Stop begging for clarity while consuming confusion. Change your intake, and your output will follow. Next up: we'll dive into that healthy soul-nutrition plan. Because no amount of healing can stick if your daily intake is toxic.

Daily Soul Nutrition: Prayer, Word, Community, Silence

Your spirit, like your body, can't thrive on an accidental diet. If you eat whatever's convenient, you'll eventually feel weak, tired, and out of sync with what your body needs. The same goes for your soul. A scattered spiritual life leads to scattered results. What you put in consistently is what you'll have strength to pull from in crisis. And if you're only feeding your faith in emergencies, don't be surprised when it doesn't have the stamina to carry you.

Prayer. Word. Community. Silence.

These aren't optional toppings. They're staples. They are your soul's vitamins, minerals, protein, and water. Without them, your spiritual immune system crashes. You become more vulnerable to offense, to deception, to burnout, to sin. These four things are your daily prescription and skipping them has side effects.

Prayer: The Soul's Breath

Let's start with **prayer**. If you only breathe when it's convenient, you'll pass out. If you only pray when you're panicking, your relationship with God becomes a 9-1-1 call, not a conversation. We treat prayer like a panic button instead of the pipeline to presence.

But **1 Thessalonians 5:17 (NIV)** gives us a challenge that's as simple as it is powerful: "Pray continually." Not perfectly. Not performatively. But *continually*. That means throughout your day, not just on your knees. In the car. On your lunch break. Before the text. After the meeting. It means praying like you breathe, naturally and frequently.

Not just deep, emotional prayers, but short ones too:

- "God, help me focus."
- "Jesus, give me grace for this person."
- "Holy Spirit, check my attitude."

These are nutritional prayers. They may seem small, but over time, they keep your spirit aligned. They keep your internal world from spiraling when your external world gets loud. Prayer is how you keep your soul clean in a cluttered world. It's not about the length of the prayer; it's about the life in it.

The Word: Daily Bread, Not Occasional Dessert

Next is the *Word*. If prayer is your breath, then Scripture is your food. Jesus said in **Matthew 4:4**, *"Man shall not live on bread alone, but on every word that comes from the mouth of God."*

The Word is not a motivational quote. It's not your backup plan when the podcast doesn't hit. It's not a dusty emergency manual. It is *living*, and it's the only thing that can speak to your soul with surgical precision. **Hebrews 4:12 (NIV)** puts it this way: "For the word of God is alive and active. Sharper than any double-edged sword... it judges the thoughts and attitudes of the heart." Without the Word, your emotions become your GPS. Without the Word, your spiritual ears stay clogged with opinion, preference, and culture. But when you're rooted in Scripture, your discernment sharpens. Your identity stabilizes. Your prayers deepen. And your obedience becomes less about feeling and more about faith.

Daily intake matters. If you only eat once a week, let's say, on Sunday, you'll starve by Tuesday. The same is true with Scripture. Five minutes a day in the Word with hunger will take you further than an hour-long binge with no intention to apply. Make it digestible. One Psalm. One parable. One verse you meditate on, not just skim. Memorize. Journal. Ask questions. Engage with it like it's alive, because it is.

Community: Your Healing Is Connected To Others

Then there's **community**. This one sting because many people want *God's healing* without *God's people*. But the prescription is clear: you don't get to grow in isolation. God designed your transformation to be connected to the body. **James 5:16 (NIV)** says, "Therefore, confess your sins to each other and pray for each other so that you may be healed."

Did you catch that? *Healed.* Not forgiven, that's between you and

God. But *healed*, that comes when you open with others. That means you don't get wholeness by hiding. You don't get breakthrough by pretending. And you don't grow by ghosting every time someone  offends you. Community isn't perfect, but it's necessary. Iron doesn't sharpen itself.

Proverbs 27:17 says, "As iron sharpens iron, so one person sharpens another."

Spiritual isolation may feel safe, but it's sterile. No friction. No growth. No mirrors to show you the stuff God's still working on. You need people who will pray for you through your mess, not just post about it. You need people who remind you of who you are when you forget. And sometimes you need someone to say, "You're not okay, and that's okay, but let's walk this out together." And if you've been burned by community, church hurt, betrayal, spiritual manipulation, hear this: *Don't let your pain become your prison.* Healing in community doesn't mean returning to the same dysfunction. It means choosing *healthy* connections. It means risking vulnerability again, not for performance, but for purpose.

Silence: The Space Where God Speaks The Loudest

Finally, *silence*. This one's hard in a world of constant noise. Silence is a forgotten spiritual discipline, one that doesn't look like much on the surface but works wonders underneath.

Psalm 46:10 reminds us: *"Be still and know that I am God."* Stillness isn't weakness. Its strength is under control. Silence is where your soul detoxes from everything else that's trying to define you. In the quiet, you start hearing what you've been too distracted to notice. Conviction has space to surface. Peace has room to settle. And God's whisper becomes clearer than your anxiety's shout.

You cannot be spiritually healthy without moments of holy pause. Turn off the phone. Shut the laptop. Sit in a room without filling it with sound. You don't have to make anything happen. You just have to *be* in His presence. Inhale grace. Exhale performance. Let the silence hold space for healing.

Sometimes silence will confront you before it comforts you, because it reveals what's there. But don't run from it. Embrace it. It's in the stillness that God often performs His deepest surgeries. That's where He uncovers motives, speaks to your identity, and reminds you that *you're loved without earning it.*

These four rhythms, prayer, Word, community, silence, are not glamorous. They're not flashy. They won't go viral. But they will *root you.* They will stabilize your walk when storms hit. They will build resilience into your spirit. They will keep your soul nourished when everything around you feels empty.

If your spiritual life is weak, don't start with more hype. Start with nutrition. Start with soul food. Start with the basics, done consistently. Because growth doesn't come from what you do occasionally. It comes from what you prioritize *daily.*

Detox Days, Choosing What To Fast From

In the physical world, a detox clears out what doesn't belong, sugar, processed chemicals, toxins, and buildup from years of eating whatever tasted good but didn't do you any good. Spiritually, it's no different. Your soul, too, collects buildup. And whether you realize it or not, your spirit can become clogged with things God never intended for you to carry opinions that don't align with truth, media that muddles your clarity, relationships that contaminate your calling, habits that hinder your holiness.

That's why spiritual detoxing isn't optional, it's essential. But here's the twist: a fast isn't just about *what you stop doing*. It's about *why you stop doing it*. It's not a spiritual hunger strike. It's a soul surgery, removing what's numbing you so you can hear God again.

When we talk about fasting in church, people often immediately think of food. And yes, that's valid, Jesus Himself fasted from food. But in today's age, some of the most toxic things we consume don't come with calories. They come with a Wi-Fi signal. They come with a "like" button. They come in the form of constant validation loops, comparison traps, mental overstimulation, and unhealed emotional attachments disguised as relationships. So, let's reimagine what a *detox day* could look like.

1. *Fast from Distraction*

Let's be real. Our attention spans are short. We can't sit in silence without reaching for a screen. We scroll through 15 different voices before we ever listen for God's. You don't need to move to a monastery, but you might need to take a day to detox from digital noise. Turn the phone off. Not silent. *Off.* Shut the tabs. Delete the app for the day. Get quiet. Let your mind feel the discomfort of silence, that's usually where God begins to speak again. **Zechariah 2:13 (NIV)** says, "Be still before the Lord, all mankind, because He has roused Himself from His holy dwelling." God is ready to move, but we often miss it because we're too distracted to notice. Fasting from distraction opens the ears of your spirit.

2. *Fast from Comparison*

Comparison is soul poison with a shiny label. It's dressed up like motivation. It sounds like "I'm just trying to be inspired." But it's slowly eroding your identity. One of the healthiest fasts you can take is from the habit of measuring your life against someone else's highlight reel. That includes the influence whose life makes you feel behind. That includes the ministry you secretly envy. That includes the person who always seems "more spiritual" than you. **Galatians 6:4-5 (MSG)** puts it like this: "Make a careful exploration of who you are and the work you have been given and then sink yourself into that. Don't be impressed with yourself. Don't compare yourself with others."

A comparison fast resets your soul back to your original design, not their version, not your imagined upgrade, just your God-given assignment.

<u>3. *Fast from Approval Addiction*</u>

This one hurts a little, but if you live for their applause, you'll die by their silence. The fast from people-pleasing might be the hardest, but it's also the most freeing. Some of us haven't heard God clearly in years because we're too busy editing ourselves to be palatable for everyone else. You weren't called to be digestible. You were called to be *obedient*. When you fast from seeking approval, you rediscover the voice of God. Isaiah 2:22 (NIV) says, "Stop trusting in mere humans, who have but a breath in their nostrils. Why hold them in esteem?" Let that verse cut. Let it detox you from your addiction to applause.

<u>4. *Fast From Emotional Crutches*</u>

That person you always text when you're lonely, but you know they're no good for your spirit. That habit you default to when life feels overwhelming, even though it disconnects you from your source. That playlist you turn on when you're sad, knowing it only feeds the sadness? It's time for a detox. Emotional crutches are convenient. But healing won't happen while you're still limping with the help of things that keep you stuck. Fasting from those crutches forces your spirit to lean into the discomfort long enough for God to meet you there. Lamentations 3:25-26 (NIV) says, "The Lord is good to those whose hope is in Him, to the one who seeks

Him; it is good to wait quietly for the salvation of the Lord." Sometimes your detox isn't about subtraction, but stillness.

The Detox Prescription

Here's your practical, non-aesthetic, real-life detox prescription:
- Choose one day this week.
- Pick one soul toxin too fast from: distraction, comparison, approval, or emotional crutches.
- Replace it with something holy: Scripture, solitude, worship, or journaling.
- Don't post about it. Don't announce it. Just *do* it.
- Sit with discomfort. Let God speak through the silence.

Because here's the truth, you can't keep praying for peace while feeding on chaos. You can't cry out for healing while binging on the very toxins that infected you. A spiritual detox isn't cute. It's messy. It's convicting. But it's the only way to make room for the Holy Spirit to move again.

Faith Clinic Reflection Page

Vital Signs Check-In • Detox Day Report • Soul Nutrition Tracker

SPIRITUAL JUNK FOOD LOG

List out the things that may be blocking your growth. Be honest. No filters, no shame, just clarity.

1. What are the toxic thought patterns you keep feeding on?

____

____

____

2. Who or what are you constantly consuming that's draining you instead of nourishing you?

____

____

____

____

3. Where have you been "snacking" on validation, gossip, comparison, or control?

____

____

____

____

4. What habits have replaced your hunger for God's presence?

____

____

____

🍽 DAILY SOUL NUTRITION TRACKER

Rate your current intake of what truly feeds your spirit (1 = starving, 5 = full & thriving).

Spiritual Nutrient	Rating (1–5)	Notes (What's missing, what needs more)
Prayer (conversation, not just requests)		
The Word (real study, not scroll-quote devotionals)		
Community (real ones, not just "hey girl" church hugs)		
Silence (space to hear God without noise)		

🚨 OBEDIENCE & HEALING AUDIT

Answer the tough questions. Healing is free — staying healed costs obedience.

5.   What did God already tell you to stop doing… that you're still doing?

---

6.   What boundaries have you been ignoring?

____

____

____

7.   Are you holding onto things that God's been asking you to release?

____

____

____

____

____

____

____

8.   When was the last time you followed through on a conviction instead of just feeling bad?

____

____

____

____

____

____

____

____

____

🧠 DETOX DECLARATION

What are you choosing too fast from this week, not for diet reasons, but for delivery?

I am fasting from:

☑ Negative self-talk

☑ People-pleasing

☑ Digital distractions

☑ Emotional clutter

☑ _____________ (Fill in yours)

☑ _________

Because I believe God is healing me around:

And I want to make space for:

____

____

💊 PRAYER PRESCRIPTION

"God, cut out what's killing me. Teach me to crave what feeds my spirit, not just my ego. Help me hunger for You more than attention, applause, or control. I don't want temporary fixes, I want soul-level healing. Show me what to starve so I can be filled again. And when I'm tempted to go back to what was toxic, I remind myself: I'm not that starving soul anymore. Amen."

Chapter 6:

Conviction Isn't the Enemy, It's The Evidence

Misdiagnosed Pain

You've probably heard someone say, "I just don't want to feel bad about myself." And to that, heaven might just raise a divine eyebrow. Because in this faith clinic, the pain you're feeling might not be a red flag, it might be a healing sign.

Conviction gets a bad rap. It's often confusing with condemnation, guilt-tripping, or religious control. But conviction, real, Holy-Spirit-infused conviction, isn't about shame. It's about diagnosis. It's about identifying the spiritual infection before it spreads. It's the check-engine light of the soul that says, "Something's off under the hood." And here's what most people miss: conviction is proof that your heart still responds. That you're not numb. That heaven hasn't stopped speaking, and that the Holy Spirit still sees you as someone worth correcting, not rejecting. 

In fact, conviction is one of the clearest signs that you're loved by God. **Hebrews 12:6 (NIV)** says, *"Because the Lord disciplines the one he loves, and he chastens everyone he accepts as his son."* So, if you're feeling that uncomfortable tug, that inner tension, that "ugh, I know I shouldn't have done that" congratulations. You're spiritually alive. And God's not done working on you. Let's walk into the surgical suite of conviction and unpack why it's not your enemy, it's your evidence.

Let's be clear, conviction isn't cute. It doesn't come with soft music, a scented candle, or a Pinterest-ready journal setup. Conviction shows up like a divine gut punch, no anesthesia, no warning, no ability to pretend you didn't feel it. And that's the point. It's not meant to feel good. It's meant to wake you up. Somewhere along the way, we bought into the idea that spiritual maturity is all calm waters and quiet smiles, as if true growth comes without pressure, tension, or turbulence. But the truth is, the sharpest growth spurts often start with a sting. Conviction is not divine punishment. It's spiritual CPR. It's heaven's way of saying: *You're not dead yet. Don't flatline now.*

We confuse God's kindness for comfort and His correction for rejection. But any parent knows this, the most loving thing you can do for someone you care about is tell them the truth when they're drifting into danger. Conviction isn't God being cruel. It's Him refusing to let you settle for less than what He died to give you.

In this chapter, you're going to see conviction through new lenses, not as a sign of failure, but as evidence that you are still on the table, still being transformed, still loved too much to be left alone. You're going to see that guilt, grief, and grace are part of the same holy cycle meant to move you, not shame you. And most importantly, you're going to realize that the ache you feel in your soul is proof that God is still at work. Welcome to Chapter 6: *Conviction Isn't the Enemy, It's Evidence*

Why Feeling Bad Isn't Bad When It Leads To Change

There's a cultural lie floating around that says, "If something makes you feel bad, it must be toxic." But let's talk about real life for a moment, a fire alarm doesn't feel good either, but it might just save your life. Conviction is the fire alarm of the soul. It's uncomfortable on purpose. It's disruptive by design. When you feel the weight of your actions, the sting of regret, or the sudden recognition that your choices are out of alignment with God's truth, that feeling is not sent to ruin you, it's sent to rescue you.

Look at **2 Corinthians 7:10 (NIV***): "Godly sorrow brings repentance that leads to salvation and leaves no regret, but worldly sorrow brings death."*

Godly sorrow is not about self-hate. It's not the pit of despair that tells you you're worthless. It's the holy ache that nudges you toward the One who can clean up the mess. Worldly sorrow says, "You messed up, you're doomed." Godly sorrow says, "You messed up, but I've already made a way back for you."

Jesus didn't die so we could keep pretending we're fine. He died because we weren't. And when that realization hits you like a freight train, when you finally *feel* the gap between who you are and who you were created to be, that's grace doing surgery, not wrath throwing punches.

Conviction is evidence that your heart hasn't gone numb. That you haven't spiritually flatlined. That the Holy Spirit still has access to your soul. So, the next time you feel bad about something, don't cancel the feeling. Let it lead you to change. Let it push you into repentance. Let it move you into maturity.

We live in a culture that constantly preaches self-love, self-affirmation, and self-acceptance, and don't get it twisted, those aren't inherently bad. But when "self" becomes the idol, conviction becomes the offense. We're told anything that makes us feel "bad" must be toxic or negative. But what if it's not? What if feeling "bad" is what leads to something *better*?

Conviction doesn't just expose sin; it exposes the invitation to healing. When you're confronted with your attitude, your pride, your compromise, or that thing you said you'd never do again but did, that sting in your spirit is not God slamming the gavel. It's the Holy Spirit extending a hand.

Let's use the example of a surgeon again. Imagine if someone had an infection and the doctor said, "You know what, I don't want you to feel bad, let's just ignore that." It would be malpractice. Healing begins with truth. And truth hurts before it helps.

King David knew this intimately. After being confronted by the prophet Nathan for his affair with Bathsheba and the murder of her husband, David didn't make excuses. He didn't defend himself. He got on his face and prayed, *"Create in me a pure heart, O God, and renew a steadfast spirit within me"* **(Psalm 51:10, NIV)**. His conviction broke him, and that brokenness became the birthplace of restoration.

The goal of conviction isn't to leave you crying in the fetal position. It's to call you back to alignment. It's a divine tap on the shoulder saying, "Hey, this isn't you. Let's come back." In a world that screams, "Don't judge me," God gently whispers, "Let Me heal you."

The Holy Spirit Isn't A Bully, He's A Better You Coach

Contrary to what some church trauma might have taught you, the Holy Spirit isn't out here with a belt in one hand and a clipboard in the other, waiting to report you. He's more like the world's best personal trainer, except instead of shouting you down for failure, He lifts you up with truth.

The Holy Spirit convicts not to crush but to coach. He's not here to belittle you but to build you into someone that looks more like Christ. Think about it: when Jesus promised the Holy Spirit in John 16, He didn't say He was sending an accuser. He said, *"When He comes, He will prove the world to be in the wrong about sin and righteousness and judgment"* **(John 16:8, NIV)**.

"Prove" here means *reveal, show, illuminate*. He's not yelling. He's pointing. He's guiding. One of the greatest pieces of evidence of spiritual maturity is how you respond to conviction. Do you get defensive? Do you shut down? Or do you lean in, knowing it's coming from a place of love?

In real-life terms, conviction might look like this:

- That awkward feeling after a gossip-filled conversation.
- Heaviness after ignoring a prompt to pray.
- That burning inside when you know you compromised your values.

You can fight it, flee it, or follow it. But make no mistake: ignoring conviction doesn't make it go away, it just hardens your heart to the signal. So, the next time you feel that holy tension rising inside, don't run from it. Thank God for it. Because it means you're not being abandoned, you're being refined. Some people avoid church or spiritual spaces altogether because they've confused the Holy Spirit with the voice of past abusers, critical parents, or manipulative leaders. They think God is standing over them with a bat and a scowl, waiting to punish every wrong move. But let's be clear: that's not conviction. That's trauma, wearing religion clothes.

The Holy Spirit is not a bully. He is not shame-based. He is not sarcastic. He is not passive-aggressive. He's not whispering, "You're trash", He's whispering, *"You're better than this."* **John 16:8 (NIV)** says: *"When He comes, He will prove the world to be in the wrong about sin and righteousness and judgment."*

That's what conviction does, it reveals, it proves, and it calls you out of denial. But it also empowers. It also equips. It also strengthens.

Think of the Holy Spirit more like a divine coach than a cosmic cop. He doesn't just tell you what you did wrong. He walks with you while you rebuild. He doesn't shame you when you miss the mark. He helps you train your aim. The Spirit convicts you because you're His. Because there's a version of you that looks more like Christ, and He's determined to pull that out of you. That might involve stretching. It might involve pruning. But it always involves love.

So, if you hear a voice that only shames, belittles, or paralyzes, it's not the Spirit. But if you feel a deep tug toward better, even when it stings, that's Him. And He's not trying to condemn you. He's calling you back to life.

How Conviction Proves You're Still Spiritually Alive

We live in a culture that glorifies numbness. "No feelings. No worries. Just vibes." But spiritually, numbness is a red flag. It's not strength, it's often a symptom of disconnection. And conviction? That sharp pinch in your spirit when something's off? That's proof your spiritual nervous system is still working.

Ephesians 4:19 warns about what happens when people lose sensitivity: *"Having lost all sensitivity, they have given themselves over to sensuality so as to indulge in every kind of impurity…"*

That verse hits hard, but it explains what's at stake. When you stop feeling conviction, it doesn't mean you're free. It might mean you've shut off the alerts. It might mean you've silently seen the alarms for so long, they no longer bother you. Conviction is spiritual proof of life. It means the Holy Spirit still has permission to speak. It means your conscience hasn't been cauterized. It means you still care about growth. And honestly? That's something to celebrate.

So, if you ever feel the sting of regret, the weight of a wrong decision, or the ache that something isn't right, pause and say thank you. It means you haven't gone spiritually numb. It means heaven is still in communication with your heart. The moment we stop feeling conviction is the moment we should worry. But if you feel it? You're still breathing. You're still His. You're still being refined.

Conviction is not spiritual rejection. It's confirmation that God's voice is still in the room. If your heart still gets stirred when you hear a sermon that hits too close to home or a scripture that interrupts your regular programming, that's not shame, that's spiritual support. Conviction isn't God trying to push you away; it's Him pulling you closer. It's His way of saying, "I still see you. I still care. I'm still working on you." 

Think of it like a spiritual check engine light. The light doesn't mean the car is total, it means something needs attention. And the worst thing you can do is ignore it, cover it up with more "busyness," or disconnect it with fake peace. The check engine light is annoying, sure, but it's also what keeps the car from breaking down completely. Conviction is your soul's version of that light. It's holy interruption, not eternal indictment.

Some of the most dangerous people spiritually are the ones who no longer feel anything. They've silenced the inner alarms so many times that now, even when the enemy has their whole soul hostage, there's no signal being sent. That's not strength, that's spiritual nerve damage.

Paul warned about this in **1 Timothy 4:2** when he said people's consciences can become "seared as with a hot iron." That's what happens when you ignore convictions for too long. It's not just that you don't feel bad, it's that you can't feel anything anymore. And while that might feel like peace for a moment, it's spiritual paralysis. You're still moving, but you're spiritually unresponsive. But if you're reading this and there's a lump in your throat, or your mind keeps going back to something you've been avoiding, or your spirit is stirring even slightly, that's *proof* you're not dead inside. That's the Holy Spirit doing His job. That's God saying, "You're still mine. I haven't given up on you."

Real conviction doesn't crush you; it confronts you. It doesn't come to condemn; it comes to correct. Jesus made that clear in John 16:8, where He explained that the Holy Spirit would come to "convict the world concerning sin and righteousness and judgment." Not to shame it. Not to guilt-trip it. But to awaken it. Conviction is how God lovingly puts His finger on the places we've tried to cover up with excuses, distractions, and spiritual procrastination.

For young people, especially, conviction can feel scary. Like you messed up and now you're disqualified. But that's not how the Kingdom works. In God's hospital, conviction is the heart monitor that proves you're still on the table. You haven't been abandoned. You haven't flatlined. He's still speaking, which means you're still worth speaking to.

The opposite of conviction is not freedom, it's numbness. Let that sink in. Feeling nothing isn't the goal. The enemy would love for you to believe that if you don't feel convicted, then you must be okay. But numbness is a symptom of spiritual decay. Just like a wound that gets infected may stop hurting, that doesn't mean its healing, it means it's dying silently. That's why God sometimes lets conviction hurt. Because He refuses to let you rot quietly.

Conviction is a sign you're still worth operating on.
Think of Peter after he denied Jesus. He didn't just cry, he wept bitterly. (**Luke 22:62**) That wasn't just emotional overload. That was conviction. That was the Holy Spirit reminding him who he was even after he acted like someone else. And you know what happened next? Jesus didn't kick Peter out. He restored him. He cooked him breakfast and re-commissioned him for ministry (**John 21**). That's what conviction does, it brings you back to the table. So, if you're feeling convicted, don't run. Lean in.

Ask God, "What are You trying to show me?" Confess the hard

truth. Cry if you need to. But don't confuse conviction with condemnation. One leads you to life. The other tries to bury you alive. And Romans 8:1 reminds us that "there is now no condemnation for those who are in Christ Jesus." That's not a pass for sin. It's a promise for grace. You are not being punished. You are being pursued. So let conviction do what it's meant to do. Let it pull you out of complacency. Let it interrupt your patterns. Let it remind you that your soul still responds. Because the worst thing that could happen is not God calling you out, it's God going silent. Conviction is His signal. Don't silence it. Don't resent it. Respond to it. Because if He's still speaking to you, that means you still belong to Him. That's not something to fear. That's something to worship about.

Guilt, Grief, And Grace, Using The Emotional Cycle For Growth

Healing is not linear. It doesn't travel in straight lines or fit nicely on a timeline. Sometimes the emotional cycle looks more like guilt, grief, grace, then back again. And that's okay. Because each part serves a divine purpose.

Guilt is the realization. It's the "oh no" moment when you see the truth. It's what Adam and Eve felt when their eyes were opened. It's not bad, it's the launchpad.

Grief is the mourning of what was lost or what was broken. It's holy sorrow. It's David writing *"Against You, and You only, have I sinned"* in **Psalm 51**. It's sitting in the ache and letting the pain teach you.

Grace is the invitation to come home anyway. It's the robe, the ring, the celebration for the prodigal, not because he earned it, but because love was waiting. This cycle, guilt, grief, grace, isn't a trap. It's a pathway. It's the soul's way of detoxing from sin and returning to joy. And the more you let yourself *feel* it instead of rushing past it, the deeper your transformation will go. You don't have to fake spiritual maturity by skipping guilt. You don't have to "faith your way" past grief. And you don't have to hustle for grace. Let each stage do what it was designed to do. Because real growth isn't rushed, it's revealed in how you let God walk you through the messy middle.

⚕ Faith Clinic Journal Page: Chapter 6, Your Conviction Check-In

Today's Spiritual Status:
(Circle one or more that describes your heart today)
- 😔 Feeling guilty
- 😨 Wrestling with grief
- 😇 Grateful for grace
- 😫 Still mad about correction
- 😵 Emotionally numb
- Awake, aware, and ready for change

🧠 Reflect + Write

1. ***What's one area where you've been feeling convicted lately?*** *(Be honest. No churchy words. Just say it like it is , even if it's messy.)* ✍ *Write below:*

____

____

____

____

____

____

2. How have you typically responded to conviction in the past?
(Circle one or more)
- Avoided it
- Over-spiritualized it
- I felt crushed by it
- Blamed someone else
- Silenced it with distractions
- Repented and realigned
- Still figuring it out

3. What would it look like to respond to conviction in a healthy, healing way right now?
(Describe a step, no matter how small, that would move you toward growth.) ✍ *Write below:*

____

____

____

____

____

🔍 Vital Check

Have you confused conviction with shame lately?
- Where did that voice come from?
- Does it lead you to change or to hide?

✍ *Answer honestly:*

____

____

____

____

____

📖 Grace Prescription

Read: Romans 2:4 (NIV) *"Or do you show contempt for the riches of his kindness, forbearance and patience, not realizing that God's kindness is intended to lead you to repentance?"*

Q: How has God shown you kindness even in your conviction?

🩹 Today's Healing Practice: The Grace List

Name three ways God has given you grace, even while you were still healing.

1. ____

2. ____

3. ____

Now take a moment to thank Him. Not because you're perfect, but because you're still in process, and conviction is proof you're still alive spiritually.

🙏 Faith Clinic Prayer

"God, I'm tired of treating conviction like a curse. Today, I see it as Your kindness pulling me back into alignment. Heal the places where I've been numb, resistant, or ashamed. I choose to let conviction be a scalpel, not a sledgehammer, cutting only what's infected and leaving behind what's whole. Teach me to hear You in correction, and help me respond with obedience, not fear. Thank You for not leaving me the same. In Jesus' name, amen."

🩺 Final Thought

Conviction isn't proof you've failed. It's proof you're being loved too deeply to stay stuck. So, stop running from the diagnosis. Start responding to the treatment.

📝 *Your healing isn't over, it's just beginning.*

Reflections

____

____

____

____

____

____

____

____

____

____

____

____

Chapter 7:

Get Off The Table,
Now Walk This Out

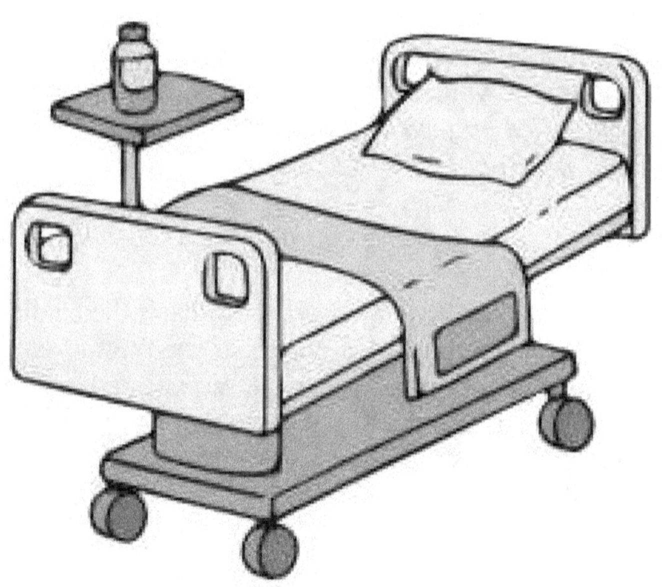

A Powerful, Engaging Introduction

At some point, the IV drip stops. The beeping monitors are quiet. The medical team is stepping back. Not because the surgery didn't work, but because now it's time for you to *move*. Welcome to the part of your faithful journey where your healing has already happened in heaven, and now it needs to show up in your habits. 

This is the chapter where we tell you: you're no longer patient. You're the one carrying the prescription. And before you reach for another prayer for breakthrough or lay down for another round of "God, fix me," the Spirit is handing you your discharge papers and saying, *"Now walk it out."*

Healing is holy, but healing is also a beginning. Jesus didn't heal people so they could sit around admiring the bandages. He healed them so they could live whole. In **John 5**, He told the man at the pool of Bethesda, *"Pick up your mat and walk."* Notice, He didn't say *"sit there and write about how deep your healing was."*

Nope.

He said, "Get up. Move. *Go live different.* And that's the challenge for many of us in the Church. We've gotten so used to the surgery table; we've turned healing into a lifestyle. We've made spiritual recovery a permanent address instead of a pitstop. But healing was never the destination. It was the doorway. And now God is calling you to walk through it.

This chapter is for the ones who know too much now to keep laying down. The ones who have seen God's scalpel work, who've cried through the cutting, and who now feel the itch of stitches telling them: it's time to move. You've done the pain table. You've wrestled with conviction. You've detoxed your soul and thrown out the spiritual junk food. And now, it's time to walk this faith *out* like you believe it.

Doing Faith Instead Of Studying It To Death

Let's be real, some of us are spiritual scholars who don't do what we study. We know all the verses on grace but still walk around carrying shame. We've memorized entire chapters of Romans but can't forgive the person who ghosted us last summer. We've got notebooks filled with sermon notes, highlighted Bibles, downloaded devotionals, podcasts on queue… and yet, our actual *life* looks the same week after week.

This is the danger of *spiritual paralysis by analysis*. We've convinced ourselves that *learning* is the same as *obeying*, but **James 1:22** calls us out hard: *"Do not merely listen to the word and so deceive yourselves. Do what it says."*

Let that sink in, you can deceive yourself by being a good listener if you're also not a doer.

It's like going to the gym five days a week, watching fitness videos, talking macros and protein intake with your trainer… and never lifting a single weight. You'd walk out feeling productive, but your body would stay the same. The Word is meant to be lived, not just learned.

The *Faith Clinic* wasn't just a masterclass in spiritual healing. It was the beginning of your spiritual rehab. And guess what? Rehab is hard. It's uncomfortable. It requires motion. You must train your muscles again, not just physical ones, but soul ones. You must learn to stretch your patience, build endurance in prayer, strengthen your obedience.

Jesus isn't asking you to know more, He's asking you to live what you already know. So, the next time you feel the urge to take *one more* course, or *one more* devotional, or *one more* YouTube sermon before you act on what God told you 6 months ago… remember this: **discipleship isn't just study, it's movement.**

Discharge Instructions From The Faith Clinic

If this journey were a real hospital stay, the nurse would hand you a clipboard with follow-up instructions before they let you leave.

It would say things like:

- Take your meds every day.
- Avoid heavy lifting for 6 weeks.
- Come back for your check-up in 3 months.
- Call us if anything feels off.

Spiritually? Same concept.

Here's your Faith Clinic discharge sheet:

1. Stay in the Word like it's your prescription refill.
You don't stop reading the Bible just because you feel better. Healing is maintained by feeding your spirit consistently. Your daily dose of Scripture is what keeps your new heart healthy.

2. Guard your environment.
Don't return to the toxic environments that made you sick in the first place. You don't leave the hospital and go straight back into mold. God pulled you out of that crowd, that relationship, that cycle, don't check back in because it's "comfortable."

3. Stay connected to the body.
You weren't meant to recover alone. The Church is supposed to be your rehab center. Not perfect people, but people who push you to keep going when the limp is real. Hebrews 10:25 says, "Do not give up meeting together… but encourage one another." Isolation is an infection waiting to happen.

4. Watch for symptoms of relapse.

Are you snapping more? Numbing out again? Avoid prayer? Comparing your journey online? These are signs. Pay attention. Don't shame yourself, but don't ignore the indicators either. Call your spiritual doctor (aka your mentor, accountability partner, or Jesus directly).

5. Keep showing up, especially when you don't feel it.

Faith isn't about feeling. It's about fidelity. If He's your Healer, stay under His care, not just when it hurts, but when you're walking whole.

You're Not A Patient Anymore, You're In The Rehab Phase Now

You made it off the table. The surgery worked. And now, it's not about healing. It's about building a lifestyle around that healing.

In **Luke 17:14**, Jesus heals ten lepers, but only one comes back to thank Him. Here's what's wild: He healed all ten, but only one was made *whole*. There's a difference. The nine people experienced *change* in their condition, but the one who returned experienced *transformation* in his relationship. You've experienced healing. The question now is: Will you walk in wholeness?

Rehab is what teaches you how. It's where the scar tissue starts to soften. It's where the Holy Spirit teaches you to walk again, not with old habits and survival modes, but with new rhythms of grace. You don't need anesthesia anymore. You need *discipline*. You need *daily surrender*. You need *faith reps*.

Faith doesn't stay strong on its own. You have got to train it. And rehab is where you put in the reps: praying even when you're tired, forgiving when it feels unfair, staying committed when you're tempted to ghost the process.

Rehab isn't glamorous. No lights. No crowd. No platform. Just you, your new heart, and a God who walks every step with you.

So, stop trying to sneak back into the emergency room every time you feel unsteady. The surgery's done. The discharge is signed. You're not broken anymore, you're rebuilding. You're walking. You're whole. Now I'm going to live like it.

⚕ Faith Clinic Reflection Page

1.   **What did I learn about myself in this chapter?**
     (Think about your current posture. Are you still lying on the table, waiting for healing, or have you started walking out your faith in action?

____

____

____

2.   **What patterns have I been stuck in that this chapter exposed?**
     (Consider places where you've been more of a patient than a participant.)

____

____

____

3.   **What does "rehab faith" look like for me right now?**
     (Walking out your faith daily is different from the emergency room phase. Are you strengthening your spiritual muscles?)

____

____

____

____

4. **How can I tell if I've been studying faith more than living it?**
    (Look at your calendar, habits, and community. Are they built on applied truth or just accumulated knowledge?)

____

____

____

5. **What does God want me to start doing that I've been delaying?**
    (Delayed obedience is still disobedience. Use this space to be honest.)

____

____

____

____

____

6. **What "discharge instructions" am I taking away from this chapter?**

---

7. (Write out the habits, mindsets, or disciplines you believe the Holy Spirit is prescribing now.)

📃 Faith Clinic Journal Page

Vitals Check Before You Go:

🩹 **Today's Pain Point**:

(What did God touch today that still feels a little sore?)

💊 **What's My Prescription Today?**

(Summarize what you believe God is telling you to DO, not just think about.)

🏃 **What Step Am I Taking This Week to "Walk It Out"?**

(Describe the next actionable step. Be specific.)

💬 **Who Will I Be Accountable to?**

(Healing grows faster when witnessed. Write a name. Schedule a check-in.)

📖 **Scripture to Stand On:**

(Choose a verse that keeps your spiritual legs strong when you're tempted to lay back down.)

🧠 **What Lies Am I Leaving on the Table?**

(You don't need that fear, shame, or apathy. Write it down. Call it out.)

✏️ Prayer Activation

"God, I know You didn't heal me just to have me sit here. I know I've been on the table for a while, letting You work on me. But now You're calling me to rise. I won't confuse rest with inactivity. I will

walk. I will obey. I will move on purpose, no longer as the patient, but as the healed. Show me how to rehab my faith and live like someone who made it out of surgery. In Jesus' name, Amen."

Reflections

Chapter 8:

When Healing Feels Like Losing Everything

Letting Go Of The Old You

There's something nobody tells you at the altar call: healing comes with funerals. And not just the kind where people bring casseroles and awkward condolences, but the kind where *you* must bury parts of yourself you thought were permanent. When God begins a healing work, He doesn't just apply balm to your bruises. He starts removing everything infected, habits, identities, titles, roles, relationships, and yes, even your sense of who you were. Letting go of the "old you" aren't just uncomfortable; it feels like dying because, in a very real spiritual sense, it is.

That version of you who knew how to survive dysfunction? Gone. The part of you who used sarcasm to shield trauma. Dismantled. The identity built around performance, people-pleasing, hustle, and hyper-independence. Evicted. You prayed for God to heal you, but now you're looking around your life wondering what's left. Where did everyone go? Why do you feel like a stranger in your own skin?

But here's the truth: the *old you* can't inherit *new healing*. The healed version of you isn't coming to bandage over what was, it's built from the ashes of what no longer serves God's purpose in your life. Letting go feel violent because it shakes your internal attachments. But when Jesus said, "Whoever wants to save their life will lose it, but whoever loses their life for me will find it" (**Matthew 16:25** NIV), He wasn't talking about a hypothetical martyr's death. He meant *this*: surrendering what was never whole in the first place so you can finally be.

This is why healing often feels cruel. It's not because God is harsh, it's because we've been holding tightly to what's killing us. And when God starts removing it, our first instinct is to mourn the loss, not recognize the rescue.

The Breakdown Before the Breakthrough and nobody warns you that healing sometimes feels like demolition. That before God rebuilds, He often tears down. Before joy comes, loss usually knocks first. We want resurrection, but without the cross. Transformation, but without the shedding. We want the "after" picture with none of the "before" pain. But in the *Faith Clinic*, here's what we've learned: healing is not just about feeling better. It's about becoming whole, and becoming whole means shedding what doesn't fit your new identity anymore. The toxic mindsets. The broken relationships. The approval addiction. The codependency dressed in "ministry."

The habits that comforted your dysfunction but suffocated your destiny. Yeah, all of that? It's got to go. And the letting go? That's the part that feels like loss. That's the part nobody claps for. That's the quiet funeral for the version of you that learned how to survive in chaos, you that hustled for love, you that made peace with shame, you that kept praying to be healed while secretly holding onto what broke you. 

Healing will not let you stay the same. And in that moment, when everything starts falling away and people don't understand and even if you aren't sure who you are anymore, it won't feel like healing. It'll feel like losing. Like being stripped. Like being abandoned. Like God just turned off the lights in the middle of your story. But that's where faith begins to speak, this isn't punishment, it's pruning. This isn't rejection, it's redirection. This isn't you falling apart, it's God pulling out the rot so you can finally grow.
Let's dive in.

Pruning, Not Punishment

There's a difference between being punished and being pruned, but when the blade is in motion, it's hard to tell the difference. Many of us, especially those raised in rigid religious environments, have learned to associate discomfort with divine disapproval. So, when God starts cutting away what's no longer fruitful, our default is to ask, *What did I do wrong?* But pruning isn't punishment. It's preparation.

In **John 15:2 (NIV),** Jesus says, *"He cuts off every branch in me that bears no fruit, while every branch that does bear fruit, he prunes so that it will be even more fruitful."* That means the very evidence that God *is* with you might be the pain you're trying to pray away. God prunes not to hurt you, but to make space for growth that can't happen any other way.

Think about it, a plant can't decide what stays or goes. It trusts the gardener. And yet we, as God's vines, try to negotiate our pruning schedule. "Lord, cut this, but not that. Heal me but leave this person. Deliver me but let me keep this coping mechanism." We want fruitfulness without surrender, healing without the discomfort of divine surgery.

But spiritual pruning means cutting off the things that drain us, even when they look alive. And sometimes that means God removes something we *loved*, not because it was inherently bad, but because it was blocking the sunlight from something better. Don't confuse removal with rejection. It's not that God is mad, it's that He's more invested in your purpose than your comfort.

Healing means accepting cuts. You're not being punished. You're being made fruitful. Pruning always looks violent to the untrained eye. You see a branch being cut back and assume something's wrong. But a good gardener knows pruning isn't about discipline, it's about destiny.

In **John 15:2 (NIV),** Jesus said: *"He cuts off every branch in Me that bears no fruit, while every branch that does bear fruit, He prunes so that it will be even more fruitful."*

Did you catch that? The fruitful branches get *cut*, too. You can be doing everything right, growing in faith, loving others, seeking God, and still, you feel like things are falling away. Why? Because growth isn't about comfort. It's about alignment.

God prunes because He sees what's ahead. He knows what habits, connections, distractions, and even good things will limit your ability to go further. So, He cuts. And when He cuts, it often feels like loss.

Youth often struggle here. You finally get into a friend group, and suddenly things shift. You start living for Christ, and relationships change. You start pursuing healing, and your phone gets a little quieter. It feels like abandonment, but it's divine protection.

God doesn't just heal wounds; He removes what causes them. That breakup you cried over. God saw where it would've taken you. That opportunity you didn't get. God saw what it would've cost you. That friend who ghosted you? Maybe they weren't equipped to go where you're going.

So next time something leaves, instead of assuming it's punishment, ask: *What is God preparing me for that I can't see yet?* Because pruning isn't personal loss, it's prophetic preparation.

Why It Feels Like Isolation Before It Feels Like Peace

No one warns you that healing might be the loneliest chapter of your story. Before the peace comes, there's usually a purge. And in that in-between space, you feel like you're floating, disconnected from your old life but not yet rooted in your new one. This is the part of the faith clinic where the waiting room feels like a wilderness.

People start to disappear, some by God's hand, others by their own choice. Conversations dry up. Invitations slow down. You scroll your phone and realize no one checked in today. You thought healing meant finally being seen. But right now, you feel invisible. This is where the enemy starts whispering: *"See? You're not really healed. You're just alone. Nobody wants the real you. God's punishing you."* But isolation isn't always abandoned. Sometimes, it's a sacred separation. God clears the room so He can be the loudest voice again.

Even Jesus, before beginning His ministry, was led *into* the wilderness by the Spirit (**Matthew 4:1**). Why? Because intimacy with God is forged in the quiet places. And healing, real healing, often requires that every other voice gets silent so you can finally hear His.

Peace isn't the absence of noise; it's the presence of God. And sometimes, He needs you alone so you can recognize that His presence *is* peace.

Healing is lonely sometimes. Because when God starts the surgery, He often clears the room. People won't understand your healing process. Some will want the old you, the one that tolerated dysfunction, stayed quiet to keep peace, kept showing up in rooms where your soul was dying. Others will misread your boundaries as arrogance or your silence as disconnection. They'll say you've changed, and they're right. You have.

In **Mark 1:35 (NIV)**, even Jesus went off to lonely places to pray. He embraced solitude before miracles. Isolation, in God's hands, becomes incubation. It's where He recalibrates your mind. Where He detoxes your soul. Where He rewires your identity. Where He speaks softly so that your roots grow deep. The noise fades so His voice can rise. But here's the hard part, in this silence, anxiety may scream louder. You may second guess yourself. You may feel like nobody sees you. But peace isn't the absence of noise, it's the presence of God in the middle of it.

Young people often make mistakes in isolation for failure. But maybe you're not being left behind, maybe you're being set apart. Maybe God removed the crowd so you could hear Him clearly. Maybe solitude isn't punishment, but positioning.

You don't get healed in a stadium. You get healed in secret, in the quiet places where God touches the wounds you tried to hide with performance. Let the quiet do its work.

God Removes What Wounds Before He Restores What Heals

A doctor doesn't bandage infected skin. They clean it. They scrape, stitch, they sometimes cut away tissue. Why? Because treating the wound without removing the infection is malpractice. And God is no negligent surgeon.

So, what feels like loss, the sudden end of friendships, the exposure of hidden sin, the unraveling of your plans, might be the beginning of His healing. Sometimes, what breaks your heart is the very thing that saves your life.

Exodus 14:13–14 (NIV) reminds us: *"Do not be afraid. Stand firm and you will see the deliverance the Lord will bring you today… The Lord will fight for you; you need only to be still."*

Stillness isn't passivity. It's surrender. It's letting God clear the infection, pride, performance, people-pleasing, trauma identities, before He applies the balm. And here's what you'll learn: restoration isn't about returning to what you were before. It's about becoming what you were always meant to be. The job you lost. Maybe it was killing your creativity. The relationship that ended? Maybe it was silencing your identity. The plan that failed? Maybe it was too small for the calling on your life.

 God doesn't remove just to grieve you; He removes to grow you. So, stop mourning what God is replacing. Let Him clean the wound, remove the rot, and build the healing on clean ground. Because the best part of healing? It is realizing you're becoming someone you never imagined but always hoped for. If you've ever begged God to "just fix it," and instead He started tearing it apart, congratulations, you're not being ignored. You're being *overhauled*. God doesn't slap Band-Aids on infected wounds. He removes what's rotting so He can rebuild what's righteous.

We often ask for restoration while still clinging to what harmed us. We say, "Lord, heal me," while refusing to detach from the relationships, mindsets, or sin patterns that caused the wound in the first place. But God loves you too much to perform surface surgery. If He's removing something, it's because it no longer serves your healing.

In the Old Testament, when God promised to bring His people into a land flowing with milk and honey, He *first* drove out the nations occupying it (**Exodus 23:30**). Why? Because healing can't live where bondage still has the lease. Before God rebuilds your joy, He'll remove your idols. Before He gives you wholeness, He'll strip your dependencies. Before He speaks peacefully, He'll silence your chaos.

This process is not sabotage. It's strategy. When God takes something from you, it's not just loss, it's surgery. And while it may feel like you're being emptied, you're being *made room for*.

Healing is not about getting back what you had. It's about becoming who you were meant to be, even if that means losing everything that once made you feel safe.

⚕ Reflection Page: Truth On The Table

- What did you have to let go of in this season that you didn't expect?

____

____

____

- How has God revealed that what you thought was punishment was pruning?

____

____

____

- In your isolation, did you hear God clearer, or did you resent the silence?

____

____

____

- What wound are you still trying to protect from removal? Why?

____

____

____

____

____

- Are you allowing God to remove what no longer serves your healing, or are you holding it hostage out of fear?

____

____

____

📝 Journal Page: The Discharge Papers

1. **Write a eulogy for the version of you that can't go into the next season.** What parts of yourself must die so healing can fully live?

____

____

____

2. **List five things you thought were necessary, but God removed.** How has your faith shifted through the loss?

____

____

____

____

3.   **Finish this sentence:** "I used to think healing looked like _____________. But now I know it means _______________."

4.   **Describe your current wilderness.** What are you learning about God when the crowd is gone?

____

____

____

5.   **Write a prayer of gratitude for what God removed, even if it still hurts.** Trust that healing *never subtracts without intending to add.*

____

____

____

____

____

____

____

____

____

____

____

____

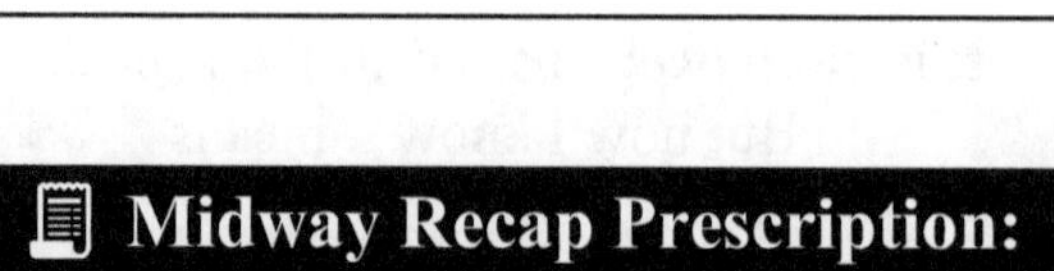

Patient Name: [Insert Yours Here]

Spiritual Chart #: 777-GRACE

Date of Admittance: The moment you asked God to heal more than just your feelings.

Primary Diagnosis: Chronic Comfort Addiction with Acute Avoidance of Conviction

Specialist Assigned: The Holy Spirit, M.D. (Master Deliverer)

♀ <u>Chapter 1</u>: Welcome to the Pain Table, This Won't Be Comfortable

Symptoms on arrival: Religious numbness. Expectation of a feel-good faith experience.

Treatment administered: Reality Check IV. You walked into the clinic thinking it was a spa and got strapped to a surgical table instead.

Key Insight: Healing doesn't start with comfort. It starts with confrontation. You can't restore it until you admit what's broken.

Prescription: Stop asking for a quick fix and prepare for surgery.

⚲ Chapter 2: Open Heart Surgery, Cutting Through the Numbness

Symptoms addressed: Pretending you're spiritually "fine." Habitual faking.

Surgical procedure: God cracked your chest open to reveal what you've been hiding.

Key Insight: Conviction is not cruelty, it's clarity. The Holy Spirit doesn't sugarcoat truth just to keep your feelings comfortable.

Prescription: Trade your hashtags for heart work. Recovery begins with honesty.

⚲ Chapter 3: Scars Are Proof That Surgery Worked, Stop Hiding Them

Symptoms addressed: Shame over past wounds.

Wound care strategy: Reframing scars as testimonies instead of liabilities.

Key Insight: God doesn't erase your scars; He exposes them to help someone else heal.

Prescription: Show your healed places. Your past no longer has authority, but your healing does.

⚲ Chapter 4: Spiritual Surgery, God Doesn't Use Anesthesia

Symptoms addressed: Resisting God's process.

Procedure logged: Removal of hidden pride, idols, and internal infections.

Key Insight: God isn't trying to comfort the fake version of you, He's trying to resurrect the real one.

Prescription: Let Him cut deep. Your numbness was never the goal.

⚲ Chapter 5: Check Your Vitals, The Soul's Emergency Signals

Symptoms uncovered: Emotional shortness of breath. Critical faith fatigue.

Monitored conditions: Bitterness, burnout, spiritual malnutrition.

Key Insight: Ignoring your soul's emergency alarms only delays your healing. Vital signs matter in the spirit too.

Prescription: Monitor your reactions, they're a reflection of your spiritual condition.

♀ Chapter 6: The Recovery Room, Conviction Is a Sign You're Healing

Symptoms treated: Over-correction, self-condemnation, guilt spirals.

Treatment focus: Learning to sit with conviction without falling into shame.

Key Insight: Conviction is proof that your spiritual nerves are waking up. You're not being judged, you're being realigned.

Prescription: Stay awake in recovery. Don't confuse spiritual soreness with failure.

♀ Chapter 7: Get Off the Table, Now Walk This Out

Symptoms noted: Dependency on spiritual "caregivers." Stuck in learning mode.

Discharge instructions: It's time to walk. You're not patient anymore, you're in rehab.

Key Insight: Faith isn't something you just *study*, it's something you *do*. Healing comes with responsibility.

Prescription: Move your muscles. Apply what you've learned. Walk out your healing daily.

♀ Chapter 8: When Healing Feels Like Losing Everything

Symptoms logged: Identity crisis. Grief over what God removed.

Triage notes: You're not being abandoned, you're being redefined.

Key Insight: Healing feels like loss because the "old you" had to die. God is not punishing you; He's pruning you.
Prescription: Don't panic. What God removes, He replaces, but only after you release it.

🧠 Spiritual Status Update:

- **Emotional Honesty:** Improving
- **Conviction Response Time:** Accelerated
- **Faith Application:** In Progress
- **Religious Codependency:** Significantly Reduced
- **Holy Spirit Sensitivity:** Returning
- **Self-Deception:** Dying
- **True Healing:** Beginning

💬 Next Steps:

Patient Notes:

You've made it halfway through the clinic. Congratulations. But remember halfway healed is not healed. Don't climb off the operating table prematurely. Don't frame your discharge papers until obedience becomes your daily rhythm. The rest of this journey? It's not just about surviving surgery; it's about living as someone who's been *completely transformed.*

Reflections

____

____

____

____

PERSONAL NOTES

Chapter 9:

Group Therapy, Healing Happens In Community

Intro: Healing Was Never Supposed To Be A Solo Act

Welcome to the part of healing everyone tries to skip *other people*. We love the idea of private breakthroughs, tears behind closed doors, one-on-one sessions with God, journal entries no one sees. It's neat. Safe. Controlled. But Kingdom healing? It always gets messy, because it always involves *community*.  It was never meant to be a one-on-one appointment. It was meant to spread, collide, provoke, and transform into rooms filled with other flawed humans. That's where real growth shows up, not in your quiet time, but in your group chats, small groups, and unfiltered moments where your edges scrape against someone else's healing journey.

Here's the truth no one wants to admit people hurt you, and people will be part of what God uses to heal you. Scars made in relationships are often healed in relationships. So, if you're praying for God to make you whole but still ghosting every opportunity for accountability, connection, or vulnerability… you're not healing. You're hiding.

Faith without community isn't spiritual maturity, it's spiritual isolation in disguise. Healing happens when you sit in the circle, put your pride down, and say out loud, *"I don't have it all together, but I'm still showing up."* You don't need a stage. You need a circle. And sometimes, healing won't hit until you open enough to let someone else see the wound. Let's dig in.

Why God Never Heals You To Make You Private

Here's a hard truth wrapped in a gentle reminder: *Your healing is personal, but it was never meant to stay private.* We live in a culture that celebrates silence when it's polished, and exposure only when it's filtered. So, we treat healing like spiritual selfies crops out the messy parts, slap on a scripture, and post it when it's presentable. But that's not how God works.

 God doesn't rescue you from drowning so you can sit silently on the shore while others drown right in front of you. If He pulled you out of darkness, it was so you'd carry a lantern for someone else. If He healed you from what should've taken you out, it wasn't just to make your life easier, it was to make your life *useful*.

In Mark 5, Jesus heals a demon-possessed man, someone society chained up and left for dead. After being set free, the man begs Jesus to let him come along. Seems like a good request, right? But Jesus says no. Why? *"Go home to your own people and tell them how much the Lord has done for you, and how he has had mercy on you."* **(Mark 5:19 NIV)**.

In other words, your healing has a public assignment. That's the part we don't like. We want healing, not homework. We want deliverance, not discipleship. But God won't let you keep your breakthrough to yourself. Why? Because someone else's freedom is tied to your testimony. Your story isn't just yours anymore, it belongs to the community that needs to know how healing is possible.

Private healing with no public fruit is just spiritual hoarding. And hoarding never multiplies healing, it smothers it.

The Need For Accountability After Breakthrough

Here's the uncomfortable part nobody warns you about: after the breakthrough, you're vulnerable. You're not at the finish line. You're at the *follow-through*. That's why God doesn't just give you healing, He gives you people. *Because accountability is what keeps your freedom intact when feelings fade.*

You might've walked out of that last stronghold. You might be free from addiction, the toxic relationship, the double life. But now comes the real test: *Can you stay free when no one's watching?* That's were accountability steps in, not as a prison guard, but as a personal trainer for your soul.

We treat breakthroughs like a badge of honor. But breakthrough without discipline is like surgery without rehab. You might feel better, but you won't walk right until you train those muscles again. That's what accountability does, it strengthens the healed places so they don't rupture under pressure.

Ecclesiastes 4:9-10 (NIV) reminds us, *"Two are better than one… If either of them falls, one can help the other . But pity anyone who falls and has no one to help them up."* Translation? Healing in private might feel easier. But staying healed requires someone who can call you out when you're about to go back to what God already pulled you from. Accountability isn't just about having someone to confess to. It's about having someone who will remind you who you are when you forget.

Finding Safe People (Not Perfect People)

If you've ever said, *"I don't trust people"* we get it. Church hurt is real. Betrayal is brutal. And spiritual trauma leaves invisible bruises. But here's what you need to know: *Just because you were wounded in community doesn't mean you can heal in isolation.* It means you must be wiser about who you open to, not *if* you open. Stop looking for perfect people. Start looking for *safe* ones.

Safe people aren't those who always say the right thing, they're people who make room for your process without weaponizing your pain. They're the friends who don't flinch when you're raw, who don't gossip when you're honest, who don't abandon you when you relapse into old patterns. They don't try to be your Holy Spirit, but they also won't let you run from Him either.

Safe people have fruit. Not perfection, not polish, but *evidence* of walking with God. Look for humility. Look for people who repent quickly. Look for people who take correction without offense. Those are the ones who can hold space for your healing without projecting their brokenness onto it.

Galatians 6:1–2 (NIV) says, *"If someone is caught in a sin, you who live by the Spirit should restore that person gently… Carry each other's burdens, and in this way, you will fulfill the law of Christ."* God knew healing wouldn't be linear. That's why He told us to carry each other, not criticize each other.

Find your safe people. And if you can't, become one. Someone is praying for the kind of community you've been afraid to step into.

From "Fix Me" To "Help Me Grow"

There's a shift that happens when healing matures you stop begging God to *fix you* and start asking Him to *grow you*. One is rooted in survival. The other is rooted in transformation. And until that shift happens, you'll treat church, friendships, and even God like an emergency room, only showing up when something is bleeding.

"Fix me" is a good start. But it's not the destination. The Kingdom doesn't just hand out healing. It invites you into *maturity*. And maturity means ownership. That's why Jesus asked the lame man in **John 5**, *"Do you want to get well?"* not because He didn't know the answer, but because healing requires participation, not just prayer.

You can't keep outsourcing your growth to pastors, podcasts, or prayer calls. Growth happens when you show up to the process even when it doesn't feel urgent. It's built in the quiet mornings, the hard conversations, the accountability texts you don't want to answer. Growth doesn't say, "Fix me." Growth says, "Equip me." **Ephesians 4:15** tells us to *"grow to become in every respect the mature body of him who is the head, that is, Christ."* That's the goal. Not just better habits. Not just better Sundays. But a life that *looks like Jesus*, even when no one's clapping.

So don't settle for being a spiritual patient. Become a spiritual partner. Stop crying for healing you refuse to grow into. Ask for the grace to *stretch*, not just to survive.

⚕ Reflection Page: The Circle Is The Cure

- Have you been hiding your healing because you fear judgment or exposure?

____

____

____

- Who holds you accountable after breakthrough, or are you trying to manage it alone?

____

____

____

- Are you searching for perfect people, or have you learned how to identify *safe* ones?

____

____

____

- Have you shifted from "fix me" to "grow me"? What does that look like in your current season?

____

____

____

- In what ways are you resisting community and calling it "wisdom" when it's really fear?

____

____

____

🖉 Journal Page: The Group Session Notes

1. **Write a list of 3 people who are safe for your healing journey.** What qualities make them safe, even if they're not perfect?

____

____

____

2. **Describe a time when accountability saved you from relapsing, emotionally, spiritually, or mentally.** What did it teach you?

____

____

____

3. **Finish this sentence:** "I'm learning that healing in community looks like _____."

4. **Write a prayer of release for your fear of being seen.** Ask God to give you boldness to show up even when you feel exposed.

____

____

____

____

____

____

____

____

____

____

____

____

____

____

____

5. **Commit to one new way to grow in community this week.** Join a group, text a friend, confess something out loud. Healing multiplies when it's shared.

📖 Faith Clinic Discharge Bonus: Spiritual Group Therapy Plan

Patient Name: ___________________________

Therapy Group Assigned: *The Body of Christ, All Members Welcome*

Date of Entry into Community Healing: The moment you stopped pretending you could heal alone.

Condition: Chronic Independence with Reluctance to Trust Others

Therapy Objective: Healing through vulnerability, connection, and discipleship in community.

🧠 Treatment Overview:

Diagnosis Summary:

- Over-reliance on private healing to avoid public accountability
- Fear of judgment mistaken for discernment
- Lingering spiritual pride dressed as "I don't need people"
- Past church trauma creating isolationist faith practices
- Avoidance of confession leading to spiritual stagnation

Primary Spiritual Goals:

1. Learn to trust again, starting with safe, Spirit-led community.
2. Allow others to see your scars without shame.
3. Submit your breakthrough to accountability structures.
4. Shift from victimhood to spiritual maturity by participating in growth.
5. Build lasting, healthy connections rooted in grace and truth.

❧ Therapeutic Instructions:

☑ **Group Participation Is Mandatory for Full Healing**
Healing will stall if you continue to treat the faith journey like a solo mission. You must plug into **intentional, Spirit-filled community**. This includes:
- Small groups
- Bible studies
- Prayer partners
- Mentorship relationships
- Vulnerable, honest friendships

☑ **Confession Is a Healing Act**
As per **James 5:16 (NIV):** *"Confess your sins to each other and pray for each other so that you may be healed."* Confession isn't about performance, it's about peace. Speak about your struggles. Say your doubts. Share your slips. That's where healing accelerates.

☑ **Feedback ≠ Attack**

You will be triggered. People will get it wrong. Still, don't retreat. Feedback from safe, Spirit-led people is a prescription, not a punishment. Don't throw away your therapy because it came in a flawed package.

☑ Not Everyone Will Be a Surgeon, But Some Are Nurses

You don't need everyone to understand your journey. But God will assign a few people who can *walk with you through recovery*. Find them. Honor them. Lean on them.

☑ Consistency Is Greater Than Intensity

Weekly community > occasional spiritual bursts. Healing in group therapy happens through consistency. Show up *before* you feel like it. Growth is often invisible before it's transformative.

📋 Group Therapy Assignments:

Weekly Practice	Goal	Notes
Join a spiritual group or ministry	Build connection and visibility	Don't just attend, participate.
Share one struggle with a trusted friend	Normalize vulnerability	It doesn't have to be deep, just honest.
Ask one person for spiritual accountability	Strengthen your follow-through	Choose someone who bears fruit, not just proximity.
Pray *with* someone (not just for them)	Build spiritual intimacy	Agreement shifts atmospheres.
Check in weekly with your "growth partner"	Track healing milestones	Keep it honest. No filters.

📖 Spiritual Therapy Verses:

- **Proverbs 27:17 (NIV):** *"As iron sharpens iron, so one person sharpens another."*
- **Hebrews 10:24-25 (NIV):** *"Let us consider how we may spur one another on toward love and good deeds... not giving up meeting together... but encouraging one another."*
- **1 Thessalonians 5:11 (NIV):** *"Encourage one another and build each other up, just as in fact you are doing."*
- **Romans 12:5 (NIV):** *"In Christ we, though many, form one body, and each member belongs to all the others."*

💡 Final Warning & Encouragement:

🚨 *Warning:* Healing in isolation may feel safer, but it's slower and shakier.

🛑 *Refusing community is spiritual malpractice.*

🙌 *Encouragement:* You're not too broken to belong. You're not too healed to still need others. You are perfectly placed in a Body that grows *together*.

👣 Discharge Plan Summary:

- **Daily:** Pray for openness and discernment in your relationships.
- **Weekly:** Engage in one group setting with vulnerability.
- **Monthly:** Evaluate how your healing has grown through shared faith.
- **Long-Term:** Shift your identity from "spiritual patient" to "community disciple."

Chapter 10:
The New Normal, Conviction As A Lifestyle

When Conviction Becomes Your Comfort Zone

You made it through the surgery. You walked out of the spiritual  ICU. You limped your way through rehab, group therapy, and journaled through every scar. But now comes the part no one glamorizes, the lifestyle adjustment. Not the dramatic healing moment, but the *daily grind* of conviction. Welcome to the *new normal*.

See, most people want healing until they realize it comes with homework. Growth isn't an event, it's a rhythm. And conviction? It's not just a moment that hits during a sermon or a breakdown. It's a lifestyle. A *constant* invitation to reflect, recalibrate, and realign with God's truth, even when no one else is watching. This is where faith stops being reactive and starts being *refined*.

You no longer get to clock out. You're not a visitor in your healing anymore, you're a resident. That means God's voice doesn't just show up when you fall. It's now embedded into every decision, conversation, and thought pattern. He's not yelling at you. He's walking with you. Whispering mid-sentence. Nudging mid-scroll. Convicting mid-ego-trip. And if you're still looking for applause every time you obey… you haven't quite arrived at maturity. The new normal isn't about external recognition. It's about internal realignment, every single day.

This chapter isn't about getting "better." It's about *staying* surrendered.

Living In Constant Reflection And Recalibration

Living with conviction means living with a mirror in your spirit, and not just the kind you glance at when you want to feel good about yourself. It's a spiritual mirror that shows you the stuff no one else sees: the selfish motives behind your generosity, the pride laced in your prayers, the subtle manipulations that you call "wisdom." Conviction doesn't just hit you when you mess up big. It hums under the surface of your daily life, inviting you to *recalibrate before you crash.*

We love talking about grace, but real grace comes with adjustments. God doesn't just forgive, He transforms. And transformation requires awareness. That means reflecting often, not just reacting occasionally.

Psalm 139:23–24 (NIV) says, *"Search me, God, and know my heart; test me and know my anxious thoughts. See if there is any offensive way in me and lead me in the way everlasting."* David wasn't asking God for a one-time correction. He was asking for *constant inspection.* Why? Because awareness protects intimacy.

Conviction as a lifestyle doesn't mean walking around in self-condemnation. It means being so attuned to the Holy Spirit that you notice when your heart shifts out of alignment, and you don't wait for a fall to fix it. You repent *quickly*. You reflect *daily*. You recalibrate *constantly*. And if you're exhausted by how often you're having to correct courses, it's not because you're failing, it's because you're finally *aware*.

This is the new normal: not perfection, but proximity to God. Not behavior management, but internal awareness. You don't live from reaction anymore; you live from reflection.

No Longer Fearing Correction

Let's be honest: most of us weren't taught how to *receive* correction. We were taught how to defend ourselves, spin it, avoid it, or fall apart under it. Somewhere along the way, correction became synonymous with *rejection,* so now every time God puts His finger on something, we flinch like He's about to slap us instead of saving us. But here's the truth: *correction isn't criticism. It's care.*

 *If God's still correcting you, that means He still claims you.* **Hebrews 12:6 (NIV)** says, *"The Lord disciplines the one he loves, and he chastens everyone he accepts as his son."* So, if you're getting called out by the Holy Spirit, take a deep breath, you haven't been disowned. You're being developed.

Think about it: nobody disciplines a kid they don't love. If God lets you keep walking in the wrong direction without saying a word, *that's when you should panic.* Correction is a sign of intimacy. He's not trying to shame you; He's trying to shape you.

Here's the deeper struggle: we don't just fear correction from God; we fear it from people too. Why? Because pride wants to be right, not healed. And when we tie our worth to our performance, any feedback feels like an attack instead of a gift. But if you truly want to grow, you must *welcome* corrections, not just tolerate it.

Proverbs 12:1 (NIV) doesn't sugarcoat it: *"Whoever loves discipline loves knowledge, but whoever hates correction is stupid."* Not misunderstood. Not immature. *Stupid.* There it is. God said what He said.

Correction is like spiritual physical therapy. It stretches you in uncomfortable ways, not to break you, but to *restore function.* You might be sore after, but you'll be able to walk straighter because of it. Living in conviction means learning to say, *"Thank You, God, for catching that in me before it grew into something worse."* It means no longer seeing correction as the enemy, but as evidence that you still belong to Him. This is the new normal: you don't panic when God corrects you, you lean in.

Spiritual Maturity:
Less About Arrival, More About Awareness

Let's kill the myth once and for all: *There is no "I've made it" in the Kingdom.* No final level. No badge that says, "Certified Healed." Spiritual maturity doesn't come with a cap and gown. It comes with humility and a mirror. Every. Single. Day.

The idea that maturity is about *arriving* somewhere, being the most  anointed, the most disciplined, the most knowledgeable, is spiritual insecurity wearing a leadership mask. You can quote scripture and still manipulate people. You can serve every Sunday and still ignore God Monday through Saturday. Maturity isn't about doing more; it's about *becoming more aware.*

Awareness doesn't mean you never mess up. It means you catch it faster. It means when pride creeps in, you don't justify it, you surrender it. When your attitude is off, you don't just blame "a rough week", you repent. When conviction hits, you don't run, you recalibrate.

1 Corinthians 10:12 (NIV) gives a sobering warning: *"So, if you think you are standing firm, be careful that you don't fall!"* In other words, maturity doesn't mean you're beyond falling. It means you're paying attention to what would cause it. You don't drift into discipline, you *decide* it.

Spiritual awareness looks like:

- Check your heart after every interaction, not just the big ones.
- Asking, *"Why did that trigger me so much?"* instead of blaming the other person.
- Noticing when your prayer life becomes performance.

- Feeling the Holy Spirit's nudge mid-conversation and having the humility to *stop yourself.*

The mature ones aren't always loud. They're not always the ones holding mics or posting online prayers. Sometimes, they're the ones who cry in worship because they still feel the weight of grace. They're the ones who repent *quickly*, forgive *freely*, and obey *quietly*. This is the new normal: less striving for *spiritual status*, more sensitivity to God's voice. You're not trying to arrive. You're learning how to stay *aware*.

Staying Open Even When The Knife Is Sharp

Here's the part of healing no one wants to talk about: **sometimes, the surgery never really ends.** You thought you were done. You thought the worst was over. You thought the pain had peaked. But then God comes back with the scalpel and says, *"There's still more."* And in that moment, you have a choice, to shut down and run… or stay open and trust Him anyway.

Staying open doesn't mean you stop feeling the pain. It means you stop fighting the process. It means saying, *"God, if You're cutting again, then I trust there's something still in me that can't stay."* This is the mature posture of faith, not passive endurance, but active surrender. 

Hebrews 4:12 (NIV) says, *"For the word of God is alive and active. Sharper than any double-edged sword, it penetrates even to dividing soul and spirit... it judges the thoughts and attitudes of the heart."* So why are we surprised when God's Word hurts a little? That sword wasn't made for surface cuts. It goes *deep*, into the attitudes you've learned to disguise, into the intentions you've never said out loud.

And let's be honest, the temptation to close off is real. Especially when growth is exposing wounds you thought you had already healed. But closing off is a trauma response, not a faith moves. It's a spiritual shutdown that tells God, *"This is as far as You can go."* But the scalpel of the Spirit doesn't honor your comfort zones. It honors your calling. And your calling? It requires capacity. It requires purity. It requires pruning you didn't plan for. That's why staying open isn't just brave, it's *necessary.* You cannot walk fully on purpose if you're only willing to be partially processed. The sharpness of God's truth may cut, but it never wounds without healing.

This is the new normal: not living numb but living *open.* Saying, *"Cut what You must, Lord, just don't let me stay infected."* You don't get to control the blade. But you do get to choose to stay at the table.

℞ Reflection Page: Welcome To The Lifestyle Shift

- Are you living with spiritual awareness, or just waiting for the next "big" moment to check your heart?

____

____

____

- How do you typically respond when God corrects you, defensively, dismissively, or with humility?

____

____

____

____

- Have you confused consistency with complacency? What would it look like to walk with God *daily* in small, unseen obedience?

____

____

____

____

- What does spiritual maturity mean to you now, has that definition changed through this chapter?

____

____

____

- What's one area you've been tempted to "close off" from God recently? Why? Are you willing to stay open, even when the knife is sharp?

____

____

____

🖹 Journal Page:
Your Ongoing Prescription For Conviction

1. **Describe what "conviction as a lifestyle" means to you now.** How is it different from the emotional, moment-based conviction you used to rely on?

____

____

____

2. **Write about a moment when God corrected you recently.** What did it reveal about your heart posture, and how did you respond?

____

____

____

3. **Finish this sentence:**
    "I used to think spiritual maturity looked like _____. But now I know it looks like _____."

4. **Write a prayer asking God to keep you aware, soft, and willing.** Ask Him to sharpen your spirit, not just your knowledge.

____

____

____

____

____

____

____

5. **Set a daily spiritual rhythm for the next 7 days.** (Example: Morning reflection, evening repentance, midday Scripture meditation). Stick with it. Let it build spiritual awareness, not perfection.

Reflections

📋 Bonus Resource: Spiritual Lifestyle Assessment Worksheet

Faith Clinic Recovery File, Group Healing & Personal Growth Checkpoint

Patient Name: ______________________________

Assessment Date: ______________________________

Phase: Transition from Therapy to Lifestyle Living

Focus: Chapters 9 & 10, *Healing in Community & Living Conviction Out Loud*

<u>Part I</u>: Community Healing Recap, Group Therapy Snapshot

✔ Group Therapy Takeaways (from Chapter 9)

Rate yourself honestly (1 = needs work, 5 = strong habit):

Community Habit	Rating (1–5)	Notes
I engage regularly in spiritual community	——	
I confess struggles to safe people	——	
I maintain accountability relationships	——	
I seek spiritual feedback without offense	——	
I've stopped looking for perfect people and started looking for safe ones	——	
I share my testimony and healing journey with others	——	

Reflection Prompt: What's keeping you from going deeper in community? Is it fear, pride, disappointment, or mistrust? What's one action step you can take this week to reconnect or go deeper?

🩺 __Part II__: Lifestyle Conviction Check, Daily Alignment Tracker

✔ Conviction Habits (from Chapter 10)

Rate your current practice:

Conviction Lifestyle Trait	Rating (1–5)	Notes
I reflect daily on my heart, habits, and motives	—	
I respond quickly when the Holy Spirit convicts me	—	
I welcome correction from God and trusted people	—	
I recalibrate spiritually even when things "look fine"	—	
I stay open to God's process even when it hurts	—	
I am no longer striving for arrival — I value awareness	—	

Reflection Prompt:
When was the last time you obeyed a conviction quickly, even if it didn't make sense to others? What did it produce in your spirit?

🧠 __Part III__: Personal Breakthrough Log, Healing in Motion

🚶 **Movement Milestones:**

What has God healed in me through community?

✎. _______________________________

What habits or mindsets have I shifted by living in daily conviction? ✎. _______________________________

What was the hardest spiritual adjustment, and how did I make it through? ✎. _______________________________

Where am I still tempted to close off or numb out?

✎. _______________________________

Who are the people God has placed in my healing circle?

✎. _______________________________

🩹 <u>Part IV</u>: Follow-Up Prescription Plan, What Now?

Weekly Practice	Goal	Commitment? (Yes/No)
Join or commit deeper in a faith-based group	Grow in connection	——
Initiate one vulnerable conversation	Break isolation patterns	——
Welcome feedback from a trusted leader or friend	Embrace correction	——
Choose one spiritual discipline to develop daily (e.g., journaling, prayer walks, repentance)	Increase awareness	——
Stay open to God's continued "surgeries"	Long-term growth	——

🗨 **Final Notes From The Faith Clinic Team:**

🩺 *You are not "done" because you feel better. You are growing because you're staying open.*

🩹 *Healing was never meant to be a temporary event. It's a lifestyle of humility, connection, and awareness.*

🤝 *You don't graduate from conviction, you grow into it daily.*

🗨 *And if you ever feel lost again, remember this: God's voice didn't leave, you just need to listen closer.*

Reflections

____

____

____

____

____

____

____

____

____

____

____

Chapter 11:

Check Your Vitals, The Soul's Emergency Signals

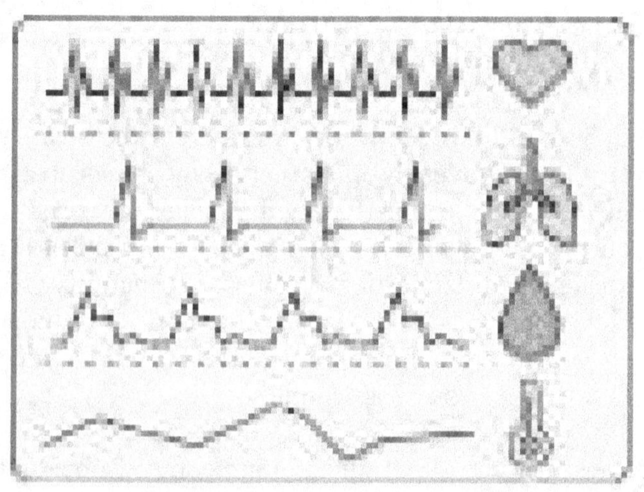

Flatline Faith, When Your Heart's Still Beating But Your Spirit's Not

You're alive, technically. Heart's pumping. Brain's functioning. Your daily checklist of school, work, bills, texts, and TikTok scrolls is intact. You show up for youth groups, you post the verse of the day, and maybe you even volunteer occasionally. But if you were honest, spiritually? You flatlined weeks ago.

 There's no pulse. No hunger. No fire. You're walking around with the motions of belief but not the movement of it. You're quoting scriptures that don't hit anymore. Prayers feel like voicemail messages to heaven. Worship songs sound like background noise instead of battles won. You say you love God, but deep down you're wondering if He left you on read.

This is what we call **flatline faith**. And here's the scary part, it doesn't always look like rebellion. Sometimes it shows up as polite, well-behaved, inoffensive Christianity that never takes risks, never asks deep questions, never reaches out, and never presses in. It's sanitized, spiritualized exhaustion disguised as maturity. It's faith that looks okay on the outside but is in critical condition underneath. Just because you're still "functioning" doesn't mean you're not spiritually fading. And you're not alone.

One of the most chilling verses in scripture comes from Revelation 3:1, when Jesus speaks to the church in Sardis: *"I know your deeds; you have a reputation of being alive, but you are dead."* (**Revelation 3:1 NIV**) Imagine that. A church with a great reputation. Probably packed out, doing outreach, singing the latest worship hits. And yet Jesus sees past the reputation into the condition, **dead inside**. He wasn't impressed by the activity. He was looking for life.

You might have a reputation, too, the good girl, the strong guy, the church kid, the "leader." But is your soul awake? Is there any real connection behind the choreography of your Christianity?

We've built an entire culture around performing like we're okay. We know the rhythm, the catchphrases, and the Instagram captions. But inside, many of us are dealing with a faith that's faint. Quiet. Struggling to breathe. You pray but feel nothing. You read but nothing sticks. You're tired but can't sleep. And when someone asks how you're doing, the default response is, "I'm fine." Let's stop lying.

Faithless Flatline Doesn't Start With Failure. It Starts With Fatigue.

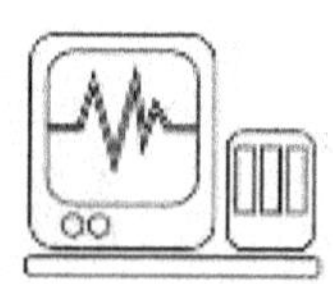 You didn't wake up one day and decide you were done with God. It happened slowly, too many distractions, too many disappointments, and not enough space to just be honest. You got caught in the grind. You got hurt but never healed. You got tired of pretending but also scared to stop. So, you stayed in the spiritual gray zone: not cold enough to walk away, but not hot enough to burn anymore. Jesus called that kind of faith lukewarm, and He didn't have gentle words for it. "Because you are lukewarm, neither hot nor cold, I am about to spit you out of my mouth." **(Revelation 3:16 NIV)**

That sounds dramatic, until you realize lukewarm faith doesn't just disappoint God, it **robs you**. It steals your joy, dulls your purpose, numbs your passion, and convinces you that survival is the same as thriving. But God never called you to spiritual autopilot. He called you to life, abundant, overflowing, soul-on-fire kind of life (John 10:10). So how do you know if you've flatlined?

Here are a few symptoms to watch for:

- You can go days without thinking about God and not feel bothered.
- You're emotionally detached in worship but emotionally reactive everywhere else.
- Conviction doesn't pierce you anymore, it just annoys you.
- You're more worried about followers than fruit.
- You compare your walk with others to justify your distance from God.
- You avoid silence, solitude, and anything that might make you *feel* something spiritually.
- You've stopped expecting God to speak.

If any of that hits you in the gut, good. That's the point. Because even though your faith may have flatlined, it's not beyond resuscitation. You might be spiritual still, but you're not spiritually done. There's breath left. There's a heartbeat waiting to be revived. And the same Jesus who spoke to dead bones in Ezekiel, the same one who shouted, "Come out!" to Lazarus, is speaking to you now. *"This is what the Sovereign Lord says to these bones: I will make breath enter you, and you will come to life."* (**Ezekiel 37:5 NIV**)

Your recovery doesn't start with doing more. It starts with being honest. Admit that you're dry. Admit that you're numb. Don't fake another prayer. Don't force another smile. Just show up, broken, bored, bitter, and barely breathing. Because that's where healing starts. Not in hype, but in honesty.

Sometimes, revival feels like CPR, it's chest-cracking, heart-pounding, spirit-jolting grace. It hurts. It shakes you awake. But it saves your life. So maybe the pain you're feeling right now is your pulse coming back. Maybe the tears you've been stuffing down are spiritual defibrillation.

You're not disqualified because you feel distant. You're not disowned because you feel dry. You're just being invited back into the presence that still has room for you. Back to the well that never runs dry. Back to the breath of God that can fill even the hollowest places. And the first step? *Tell the truth.* Stop covering up the flatline with noise and filters and spiritual jargon. God is not intimidated by your lack of passion. But He can't work with a performance. He can only heal what you're willing to expose.

So let this be your moment to check the vitals. Not your church attendance. Not your Bible app streak. Not your social media presence. Check the vitals of your soul. Is there intimacy? Is there trust? Is there a spark that still believes He's worth seeking? If the answer is "not really" don't panic. Breathe. You're still here. And that means God's not done.

The heart monitor might be weak. But if you're reading this, there's still time to return to the source. Plug back into the power. Reconnect to the only One who doesn't just revive you for a moment, He sustains you for a lifetime. And the best part? You don't have to fake a comeback. You just must want one.

Let's check your pulse. Let's speak breath into dry places. Let's invite Jesus, the real Jesus, not the version you've learned to smile through, into the room. He's not waiting to punish you for flatlining. He's here to bring you back.

Emotional Code Blue, When Anxiety, Anger, And Numbness Take Over

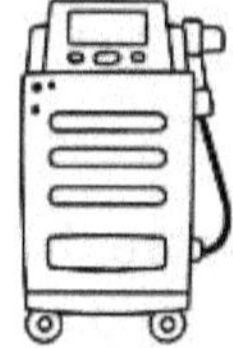

You can't always see it, but your soul can crash just like your body can. And when it does, it doesn't always come with sirens and flashing lights. Sometimes it just shows up as another sleepless night, another sarcastic post, another blow-up at someone you care about. Sometimes, it's you scrolling at 2 a.m. hoping something will numb you before the anxiety kicks back in.

Welcome to your *emotional code blue*, the part of your soul that's suffocating silently while the world keeps demanding more from you. You're not losing your mind. You're not overreacting. You're bleeding internally, spiritually speaking. And unless someone notices, unless *you* notice, you'll keep walking around functioning but fractured.

Let's break it down like we're in the ER. In medical emergencies, a "Code Blue" signals someone's vital signs are crashing, they need immediate resuscitation. No small talk. No delay. Every second counts.

Spiritually and emotionally, there's a code blue happening for too many people, especially youth. But nobody's calling the code because everyone's too busy pretending, they're "fine." The pressure to be okay is so loud that most of us miss the moment we're falling apart.

Anxiety is now in the air many teens and young adults are breathing. Anger has become the cover emotion for pain they were never taught to process. And numbness? That's the defense mechanism they've learned to adopt when the pressure to be perfect or productive gets too much to bear. Sound familiar?

Let's talk about **anxiety** first, that gnawing, unspoken pressure that sits in your chest like a weight you can't shake. It's not just nervousness before a test or butterflies before a performance. It's waking up and feeling like you've already failed, before your feet even touch the floor.

Anxiety doesn't mean you don't trust God; it means your soul is overwhelmed by a world moving too fast for your spirit to keep up. But here's what Scripture says: "When anxiety was great within me, your consolation brought me joy." **Psalm 94:19 (NIV)** It doesn't say "when anxiety was present, I got rebuked for not having enough faith." It says God brought comfort in the middle of the anxiety, not after it was over.

Now let's hit *anger,* the emotion we often weaponize because we don't know how to feel anything else. Some of us grew up in homes where crying was weak and vulnerability was punished. So, we learned to get loud instead of soft, aggressive instead of honest. But that rage? That edge? It's usually a trauma response. "Human anger does not produce the righteousness that God desires." **James 1:20 (NIV)**

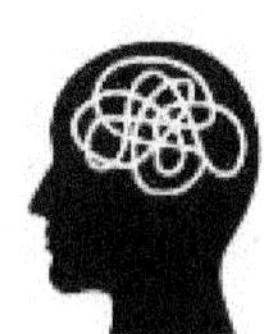

This doesn't mean you can't feel angry, even Jesus flipped tables in the temple. It means that *unhealed anger* becomes corrosive to your soul. When you're always ready to pop off, lash out, or isolate yourself, it's a sign that something inside is trying to warn you. It's not rebellion. It's the vital sign of a deeper wound. And then there's *numbness*, the most dangerous of them all. Because at least with anxiety and anger, you *feel* something. But numbness? That's when you stop caring for all together. You're still doing what's expected, but inside, it's blank. It's silence. It's a soul that's checked out.

Numbness isn't laziness, it's often *emotional burnout*. You've felt too much for too long, and your system shut down to protect you. And guess what? Even prophets got there.

In **1 Kings 19**, Elijah, the same Elijah who called down fire from heaven, ended up under a tree praying to die. Why? Because his soul was overwhelmed, and the pressure became too much. His emotional code blue looked like isolation, suicidal thoughts, and total exhaustion. But what did God do? He didn't yell at him. He didn't say, "Snap out of it." God sent an angel to feed him, let him rest, and reminded him of his purpose, *slowly*. Because even in your darkest moments, God is gentler than the world has ever been to you. Let's say it again: God doesn't cancel you for crashing. He covers you while you recover.

So, if anxiety is running your thoughts… If anger is driving your relationships… If numbness is keeping you from even praying anymore… You're not broken. You're bleeding. And bleeding people need care, not critique. So how do you start resuscitating your soul?

1. **<u>Name what you're feeling.</u>**
   Stop dumbing it down. "I'm just tired" might be "I'm afraid I'm failing." "I'm annoyed" might be "I feel invisible." Be honest.

2. **<u>Stop isolating.</u>**
   You weren't meant to bleed in silence. Tell someone. A mentor. A trusted friend. A counselor. You don't need everyone to understand, but you need someone to hear.

3. **<u>Come back to breath.</u>**
   Spiritually, prayer is breath. When you can't scream, whisper. When you can't whisper, cry. When you can't cry, sit in silence and just breathe in God's name.

"The Lord is close to the brokenhearted and saves those who are crushed in spirit." **Psalm 34:18 (NIV)**

4. **<u>Let go of the pressure to perform.</u>**
   You don't need to "get better" overnight. This is not a sprint to spiritual perfection. It's recovery. And recovery takes time.

5. **<u>Ask for spiritual CPR.</u>**
   Sometimes it's not about getting up by yourself. Sometimes it's letting others, your leaders, your community, the Holy Spirit, *press on your heart* until it beats again.

You can't wait until you're drowning to admit you're in deep. You can't wait until you're exploding to say you've been hurting. You can't keep pretending you're fine while your soul is suffocating.

This is your **Code Blue** moment, and it's okay to say you need help. Because when Jesus said He came for the sick, not the well, He meant it. And you, my friend, are not disqualified by your emotional chaos. You are the reason grace showed up in scrubs, ready to operate.

Let your emergency be the invitation. Let the crash be the call. Because there's a Healer already in the room, and He never panics when your pulse fades. He revives.

Silent Symptoms, When You're Dying Inside But No One Sees It

You're still showing up. You're still laughing at the group text. You're still serving on Sundays, posting scriptures, hitting your deadlines, and doing everything that makes people say, "Wow, you're so strong." But inside? You're barely holding on.

That's what silent symptoms do. They let you function while you're fractured. They let you show up while you're shutting down. And unless someone really looks closely, unless *you* stop and check in, you can slowly bleed out emotionally, mentally, and spiritually without ever making a sound.

We live in a world that rewards productivity and punishes honesty. It's cool to be busy, but awkward to be broken. It's fine to hustle, but weird to heal. So instead of raising your hand and saying, "Hey, I'm not okay," you play the part. You keep moving, keep performing, and keep hoping someone will notice, but not ask too many questions.

That's how spiritual cardiac arrest happens. It doesn't always start with a dramatic meltdown or a loud confession. Sometimes it looks like someone who's "fine." Sometimes it looks like the most encouraging person in the group. Sometimes it looks like the person who just got promoted to ministry. But deep down? They haven't prayed for weeks. They cry in the shower. They feel numb during worship. And they're starting to wonder if anyone would even notice if they disappeared.

This is what Jesus was talking about in **Matthew 23:27 (NIV)**: "Woe to you, teachers of the law and Pharisees, you hypocrites! You are like whitewashed tombs, which look beautiful on the outside but on the inside are full of the bones of the dead and everything unclean."

Yikes. That's not just for Pharisees; that's for anyone who's mastered *looking* holy while quietly hurting. Silent symptoms are subtle. They creep in, not crash in. And most of us miss them because we're so used to survival mode that we mistake it for normal.

Here's what silent symptoms might look like:

- You're quick to give advice, but you haven't heard God for yourself in a long time.
- You celebrate everyone else's testimony but secretly feel like miracles skip over you.
- You serve at church but avoid intimacy with God because you're afraid of what He might say.
- You isolate in the name of "rest" but it's really because community now feels exhausting.
- You say "God is good" out loud, but inside you're not so sure anymore.

Let's call it what it is: spiritual burnout in disguise. And this is where the enemy thrives, in secret. Not just sin, but *struggle*. He wants you to think you're the only one feeling like this. He wants you to think everyone else is thriving in their walk with God and you're the weak one. He wants you ashamed of the silence in your spirit, so you keep it bottled up and buried under Christian performance.

But the truth? Every believer, even the faithful, even the anointed, has had seasons of soul silence. Even David, the man after God's own heart, cried out in **Psalm 13:1**: "How long, Lord? Will you forget me forever? How long will you hide your face from me?" If King David, the giant-slayer, the worshipper, the psalmist, had moments where he felt ghosted by God, *then what makes you think you're weak for feeling the same?*

Silent symptoms aren't signs of failure; they're signs that your soul is trying to get your attention. This is your spiritual body telling you: "I need rest. I need honesty. I need God, not just the motions. I need more than noise; I need a real encounter." But how do you confront the invisible? How do you treat what no one else can see?

Start here:

1. *Confess the quiet*
Say it out loud: "I haven't heard God in a while." "I'm not okay." "I feel numb." Confession isn't about performance, it's about permission. You're giving God permission to meet you right where you are.

2. *Stop clinging to your spiritual reputation*
You don't have to be the strong one all the time. Jesus didn't come for your image; He came for your heart. And He's not intimidated by your silence. He speaks in it.

3. *Make space for sacred interruption*
Shut the phone off. Step outside. Turn the music down. Let your soul catch up with your body. Give God a chance to speak. He

doesn't always yell over the noise sometimes He whispers into stillness. "Be still and know that I am God." **Psalm 46:10 (NIV)**

4. *Let someone in*
You're not a burden. You're a human needing support. Whether it's a trusted friend, mentor, therapist, or pastor, bring someone into your silent storm. Not everyone will understand, but the right ones will sit with you in it.

5. *Do something uncomfortable and honest*
Write the journal entry you've been avoiding. Cry during worship instead of holding it in. Reach out when you feel like shutting down. Start a prayer even if it feels dry. These small acts disrupt silence with surrender. Real growth doesn't happen in the highlight reel; it happens in the dark rooms where you finally stop pretending and let the light in.

God isn't just the Savior on the stage; He's the Surgeon in the silence. And He's not asking you to scream louder or work harder. He's inviting you to collapse into Him, no performance, no polish, just presence. So, if your smile feels fake, your faith feels flat, and your soul feels like it's running on fumes, that's your spiritual symptom speaking. Don't ignore it. Don't gloss over it with a verse and a vibe.

This is your code signal. And Jesus is already walking down the hospital hallway, ready to sit with you in the silence, not to shame you, but to *revive you.* He sees what no one else does. And He loves you there.

Vital Signs Of Spiritual Recovery, What It Looks Like To Heal From The Inside Out

Recovery doesn't come with confetti. It comes with quiet shifts, often unnoticed by the crowd but unmistakable to the soul. The spiritual monitors begin to beep again, slowly, steadily, signaling that the part of you that flatlined is beginning to feel, to breathe, to believe again. This is where spiritual recovery begins.

It's not a dramatic delivery moment where everything is fixed in a flash. It's the subtle strengthening of what was once weak. It's quiet courage to try again. It's the grace to rebuild, brick by broken brick, with shaky hands and a hopeful heart.

Too many people think healing is an event. But in the Kingdom, healing is a lifestyle, a series of consistent steps, small victories, honest prayers, and Spirit-led moments that, over time, breathe life back into the places you thought were beyond repair. Let's talk about what those *vital signs* look like. Not the hype, not the hallelujahs, the real markers of spiritual recovery.

1. You crave His presence more than performance.

Where once you felt pressured to look at the part, now you're drawn to just *be* with Him. You stop comparing your walk to others and start recognizing the value of intimacy. You don't just go to church to be seen, you show up to *see* Him. Your prayer life might still be messy, but it's *yours*. And that craving? That's the Spirit's oxygen re-entering your lungs. It's Psalm 42:1 in motion: "As the deer pants for streams of water, so my soul pants for you, my God."

When you start panting for God again, not ministry, not validation, not spiritual clout, that's a sign your soul is waking up.

2. Your heart becomes teachable again.

Before recovery, everything feels like an attack. Correction feels like condemnation. Conviction feels like rejection. But when the spiritual infection clears and healing begins, your heart becomes soft again. You begin to *want* truth, even when it stings. You recognize that confrontation is not cruelty, it's care. Proverbs 12:1 (yes, this one's a little spicy) says: "Whoever loves discipline loves knowledge, but whoever hates correction is stupid." Translation: when you can receive hard truth with an open heart, you're healing.

3. *You stop bleeding on people who didn't cut you.*
Spiritual recovery means you're no longer projecting past wounds onto current people. You stop distrusting every leader because of one manipulative pastor. You stop ghosting every friend because one betrayed you. You stop flinching at love because someone else abused it. This doesn't mean you forget, it means the wound doesn't own you anymore. You learn to speak from your scars, not your scabs. You begin to build bridges instead of barbed-wire fences. And that's growth.

4. *Joy starts sneaking in again, uninvited and unforced.*
You laugh. Not the fake, "I'm fine" laugh, but the kind that surprises your mid-conversation. The kind that bubbles up unexpectedly while watching the sunset or dancing in the kitchen. You find joy in small things. You stop bracing for the next breakdown and start believing good things are allowed to happen to you. **Nehemiah 8:10** says: "The joy of the Lord is your strength." When you begin to experience joy again, not manufactured, not manipulated, you're regaining your strength.

5. *You begin to see your past differently.*
Instead of rehearsing the pain, you begin to recognize the purpose. You don't glorify the trauma, but you stop letting it define you. You start to say things like, "That season broke me, but it also built me." You realize that what happened *to* you doesn't outweigh what God is doing *in* you. **Romans 8:28** becomes more than a cliché, it becomes a comfort: "And we know that in all things God works for the good of those who love him…" Healing doesn't mean pretending the pain didn't happen. It means acknowledging that grace still got the final word.

6. *You extend grace without losing your boundaries.*

Healing gives you discernment. You forgive without foolishness. You love without losing yourself. You say "yes" with conviction and "no" with confidence. You can be kind *and* clear. That balance? That's a vital sign. It means you're not functioning from fear anymore, you're rooted in wisdom.

7. *You stop asking, "Why me?" and start asking, "What now?"*

This is a major shift. It's the difference between victimhood and victory. When you're recovering, your posture changes from questioning your past to stewarding your future. You begin to see your story as a testimony, not a tragedy. You ask God, "How can I use this?" instead of "Why did You let it happen?" This shift is sacred. It's where ministry is born.

Spiritual recovery isn't loud. It's not always visible. You won't always get applause for it. But God sees every small step. Every prayer whispered through tears. Every time you show up when you want to give up. Every wall you lower. Every truth you face. Every "amen" you say through gritted teeth. Every breath of hope you take again. That's what healing looks like. It looks like a soul learning how to live again. It looks like a heart slowly stitching itself back together under the steady hand of the Holy Surgeon. And guess what?

You're Doing Better Than You Think

So, if no one has told you lately: I see the signs. You're healing. You're not who you were. You're further along than you feel. Keep going. Keep checking your vitals. Keep surrendering to the process. Because healing isn't a destination, it's a direction. And you're headed the right way.

> ## ℞ Faith Clinic Recovery Room:
> ## Vital Signs Self-Check

"Healing isn't always loud. Sometimes it's in the quiet decision to try again." Before you move forward, let's pause and check in with your soul. Don't rush. Let this moment do what it was meant to do, diagnose what's deeper.

🔑 *Internal Temperature Check:*

1. **When was the last time you truly felt joy, not just surface-level happiness, but a deep, soul-anchoring joy?**
   - *(Write freely, even if the answer is "I don't remember." Start there.)*

2. **What does emotional or spiritual 'flatlining' look like for you?**
   - What are your warning signs?
   - What do you do when you're running on spiritual fumes?

____

____

____

____

____

3. **Have you ever caught yourself bleeding on people who didn't cut you?**
   - Be honest. What are the patterns? Who's gotten hurt unintentionally? Where do you need to pause and process?

____

____

____

____

____

____

____

4. **How do you respond to correction or conviction from God or others?**
    - Defensive? Dismissive? Teachable? Avoidant? Why?

____

____

____

____

____

5. **What does spiritual recovery look like in your life right now?**
    - Name the signs that you're healing. List them as proof for the days you doubt your progress.

____

____

____

____

____

____

📖 Scripture Meds (Read + Reflect)

- **Psalm 51:10** – *"Create in me a clean heart, O God, and renew a right spirit within me."*
- **Nehemiah 8:10** – *"The joy of the Lord is your strength."*
- **Proverbs 4:23** – *"Above all else, guard your heart, for everything you do flows from it."*
- **Romans 8:28** – *"And we know that in all things God works for the good of those who love him..."*

✒ Prescription Notes From The Holy Surgeon

Write a letter to your future self, one who's further along in the recovery process. What do you want them to remember? What truths are you holding onto today that they might need again?

____

____

____

____

____

____

____

🙏 Closing Prayer:

"God, check my vitals. Not the image I present to others, but the real pulse of my heart. If I'm flatlining, breathe into me again. If I'm wounded, don't let me walk around like I'm fine. Do the deep work. Show me how to rest. How to reset. How to listen to the signals of my soul without shame or panic. I surrender to the process, because healing with You is worth every moment of discomfort. In Jesus' name, amen."

Reflections

Epilogue
Congratulations, You've Been Discharged, Now Stay Dangerous

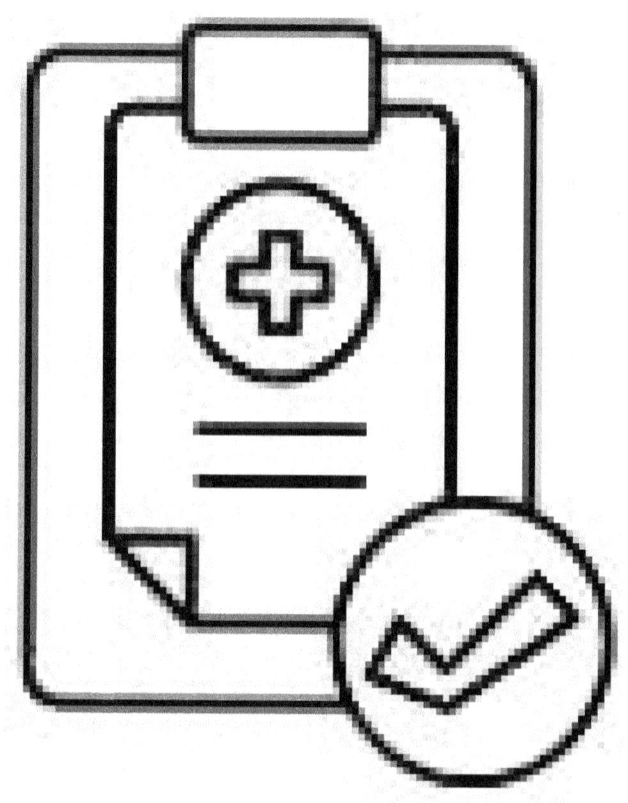

You made it. Not just through the book, but through the mirror, the knife, the silence, the purge, the group sessions, the relapse scares, the scars you finally stopped hiding, and the truths that sliced deeper than you expected.

You came for healing. But what you got was God, unfiltered, unedited, and unapologetically surgical. He didn't come with anesthesia. He came with *accuracy*. He didn't just touch the surface.

He dug through your spiritual scar tissue, your theological coping mechanisms, and your emotional calluses, until your heart remembered how to *feel* again, how to *repent* again, how to *respond* again.

And somewhere between the journals, the reflection pages, the tears you swore wouldn't fall, and the scripture that read *you* instead of the other way around… You didn't just get healed. You got ***transformed***.

Now here's the catch: this wasn't a recovery retreat. This was booting camp. This was the wake-up call for every soul that thought spiritual growth was about cute quotes and shallow prayers. This was the holy defibrillator to a heart that flatlined in religious routine. This was your spiritual rehab, and now it's time to walk *like you got up off the table.*

You don't get to unknow what God revealed in this clinic. You don't get to go back to bland Christianity or quiet disobedience. The Word that pierced you was meant to *plant something inside you.* The Holy Spirit didn't just clean the house. He took over the lease. So no, you may not have received the healing you imagined. But what you *did* receive was truth that redefined your diagnosis.

And now? You're dangerous. Because a healed believer is powerful, but a *convicted* one? That's the kind hell regrets letting survive.

🚨 What's Next? Stay In The Clinic.

This was Book One of the **Faith Clinic** series. The surgery is over, but the *discipleship* is just beginning.

Coming soon in **Book Two: "Scalpel & Sword, Healing Deeper Than You Lied About"** we're going into the *internal war zones*, the trauma you spiritualized, the cycles you renamed, the theology you weaponized to justify staying wounded.

You thought this hurt?

Wait until God starts cutting the agreements you made with your past. Because healing isn't just about what happened to you. It's about what you believed *because* of what happened to you, and who you became to survive it. So, keep your gown. Keep your journal. But next time, it will be ready. Not for a spa day. But for the battlefield that healing prepared you for. Faith Clinic isn't over. This was just your intake form. Now… go live like your healing *was worth the fight*. Discharged. But never done.

Reflections

PERSONAL NOTES

ABOUT THE AUTHOR

Dr. Patricia Tanner was born and raised in Sanford FL. She comes from a family of three siblings. Patricia Tanner is the founder of Multhai International Realty, Multhai Asset Management Services, and Multhai Investment Group which is located in Sanford, Florida. She is a graduate of the University of Central Florida, where she received a Bachelor of Science in Business Administration and a minor in Human Resources Management.

Dr. Tanner began her career shortly thereafter as a Regional Property Manager in the apartment community. Throughout her career in property management, she has built interpersonal relationships with corporate clients. She has a successful track record of increasing company revenues over $5 million annually, through hard work, commitment, creativeness, and strategic planning.

Her experience and leadership role eventually led her to achieve a Florida Real Estate Broker license. She spent fifteen years in the Real Estate field while completing a Master of Arts in Human Resources Management from Webster University, and a Master of Public Administration from Troy University. It was in this capacity that she decided to open her own brokerage company, Multhai International Realty.

In addition, Dr. Tanner finds time in her busy schedule to participate in her own Non-For-Profit Organization, Stones 2 Homes. She remains President of her organization in which she helps people build, keep, or purchase homes in affordable communities. She is the founder of PNT Property Partners in which she buys vacant land, develops it, and constructs brand new construction homes in Sanford Florida. Her overall goal is to educate and provide resources to help people overcome financial hardships and credit disadvantage to live the American Dream through homeownership in spite of economic hardship. Through her visions she will continue to grow as an entrepreneur and is willing to share her knowledge, experience, and expertise with anyone who is willing to learn.

MORE BOOKS BY THE AUTHOR

Welcome to the Faith Clinic—where your soul doesn't need to be perfect to be healed.

You've smiled through burnout. Quoted scripture while quietly unraveling. Prayed, fasted, and still felt like your faith flatlined. If that's you, Faith Clinic: Volume I is your spiritual prescription.

Dr. Patricia S. Tanner—known as The Faith Doctor—invites you into a raw, grace-filled recovery journey for the soul. With 7 powerful doses of faith-infused wisdom, this book delivers healing where performance failed and offers truth where church hurt left a scar. Designed especially for spiritually exhausted youth and young adults, each "dose" reads like an IV drip of hope for believers secretly running on empty.

You don't need to be okay to show up. You just need to be willing. The clinic is open.

NOW AVAILABLE:
www.amazon.com

Healing was just the beginning. Now it's time to grow.

If Faith Clinic Volume I met you in crisis, Volume II meets you in recovery. Because faith isn't a one-time fix—it's a lifestyle that needs maintenance, accountability, and consistency. Welcome to your follow-up care plan.

In Faith Clinic: Volume II, Dr. Patricia S. Tanner—aka The Faith Doctor—guides you through the next level of your spiritual healing journey. From navigating church trauma and burnout to facing silence from God and rediscovering purpose, this book goes deeper than devotionals. It's not about hype—it's about habits that sustain real, lasting transformation.

With raw wisdom, relatable stories, and no-shame truths, each chapter is a spiritual check-in for believers who want to thrive—not just survive. Whether you're wrestling with doubt, craving stability, or simply ready to grow up in God, this clinic is for you.

You've detoxed. Now it's time to build. Let's get you discharge-ready.

NOW AVAILABLE:
www.amazon.com

Welcome to the Faith Clinic: Anxiety Edition — where God doesn't coddle your coping mechanisms but confronts them with surgical precision.

This book is for the ones who love Jesus but still can't sleep. For the worship leaders crying in church bathrooms. For the believers who pray in spirals, fight shame on Sundays, and secretly think, "Maybe I'm the only one who can't seem to breathe through this." You're not crazy. You're just in a fight — and this book is your spiritual triage.

Inside you'll find:
- Panic attacks in pews and the prayers that still work.
- Scriptures that talk you off the ledge.
- What to do when you feel numb and God feels quiet.
- How to walk out of shame loops, judgment spirals, and performance religion.

This isn't just encouragement. It's equipment.
Because healing isn't a moment — it's a walk.

NOW AVAILABLE:

www.amazon.com

Welcome to the Faith Clinic: Stress Edition — where we don't hand you cute verses and clichés. We hand you spiritual prescriptions for real pressure, real panic, and real prayers from tired believers holding it together by a thread.

This book is for the overwhelmed—those trusting God while juggling bills, burnout, hustle culture, and holy frustration. If you've ever whispered, "God, are You even watching this mess?" this is for you.

Inside you'll find raw, soul-hitting chapters like:

- "God, I Trust You — But These Bills Keep Coming"
- "If Rest Is Holy, Why Does It Feel Like Slacking?"
- "I'm Tired of Smiling So You Won't Worry"

This isn't fluff. It's real talk for real stress—and a reminder that you're not forgotten, you're being fortified.

The Faith Clinic is open. Breathe in & take your spiritual vitamins. Healing begins here.

NOW AVAILABLE:
www.amazon.com

This isn't just a feeling — it's a flare signal from the soul. You pray, serve, and believe in God, but something deep inside is still simmering. Welcome to the Faith Clinic: Anger Edition — where suppressed emotions meet sacred intervention.

In this volume, Dr. Patricia S. Tanner guides you through spiritual triage for:

✅ Silent rage and emotional suppression

✅ The grief–anger connection

✅ Rejection wounds from childhood to church hurt

This isn't a lecture. It's a spiritual detox. No shame. No sugar-coating. Just raw, honest healing. Whether you're snapping at loved ones or silently seething under the surface, this book meets you at the boiling point—and leads you to the breakthrough.

🩺 This is the clinic.

💧 This is your moment.

And God is ready to heal the anger behind your amen.

NOW AVAILABLE:

www.amazon.com

In this powerful installment of the Faith Clinic series, Dr. Patricia S. Tanner brings biblical insight, emotional compassion, and spiritual strength to those walking through grief. Designed as a healing chamber for the soul, each "dose" of this devotional targets a different dimension of sorrow—guiding you from pain to peace, from mourning to joy.

Inside, you'll discover:

- Daily doses of Scripture-based encouragement.
- Personal reflections and prayers for each stage of grief.
- Practical faith prescriptions to help you process loss and find purpose.

Whether you are navigating the recent loss of a loved one, confronting buried grief from the past, or supporting someone else in their sorrow, this devotional offers a gentle yet powerful roadmap to healing. Come, take your seat in the Faith Clinic—where the Great Physician is ready to restore your soul.

NOW AVAILABLE:

www.amazon.com

30 Days Of Grieving

Given By The Inspiration Of God

Healing From COVID-19

Almost a year later, it hit me... My mother was gone, and I was still stuck at the hospital. I had tried everything from crying to counseling, and even prayer. Pray they told me. Trust God they insisted. But it seemed as if nothing was working. I was hurt, dealing with my reality: my mother was not coming back.

While journeying through grief, it was under the divine 'Inspiration of God' that He placed me in a trance. While I was gaining a revelation about grief, He gave me this journal, '30 Days Of Grieving.'

NOW AVAILABLE:

www.amazon.com

Can Salvation Get You Into Heaven? The Answer Is Yes! offers a powerful and biblically grounded exploration of God's eternal plan, revealing the heart of the Gospel and the assurance of salvation through Jesus Christ.

Unpacking life's most vital questions—Who is God? Why were we created? What does Jesus' life mean for us?—this book brings clarity to the believer's journey and confirms that salvation, once received, is eternally secure.

Whether you're seeking understanding or affirming your faith, this inspiring guide will lead you into the confidence and joy of knowing heaven is your eternal home.

NOW AVAILABLE:

www.amazon.com

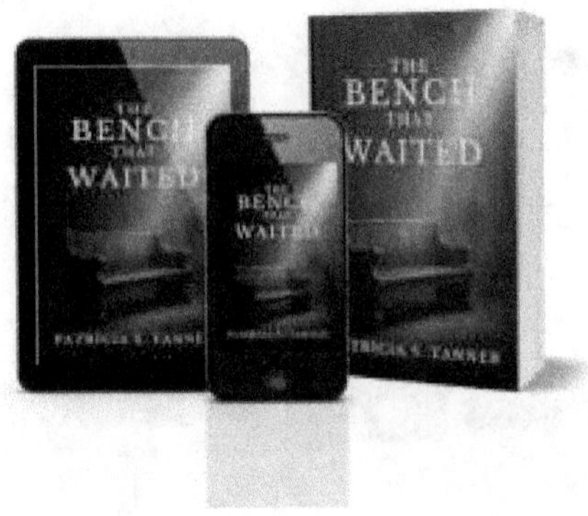

The Bench That Waited is a bold and prophetic call to action for believers who've grown comfortable in church attendance but stagnant in purpose.

With raw honesty and spiritual insight, Patricia Tanner exposes the quiet crisis of passive faith—where callings are delayed and obedience is optional.

Through Scripture, stories, and reflection, this book urges readers to rise from routine, break free from spiritual stagnation, and step boldly into their Kingdom assignment. The bench has waited long enough—will you?

NOW AVAILABLE:
www.amazon.com

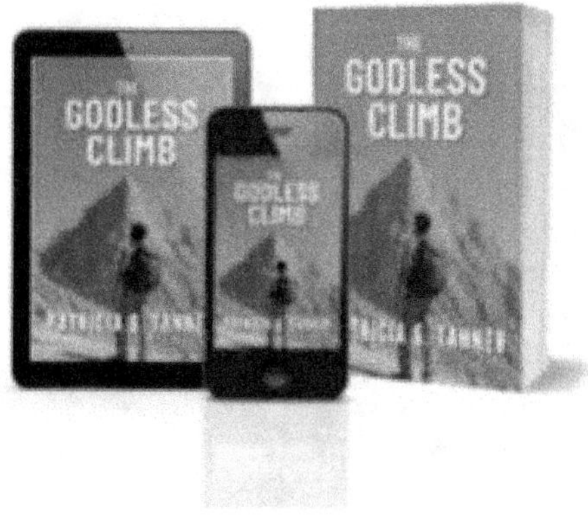

What happens when the Kingdom becomes a stranger?

The Godless Climb is not a rejection of faith—it is a raw, unflinching journey through what remains when belief unravels. With brutal honesty and tender grace, this book explores the spiritual free fall that follows the loss of divine certainty, the ache of unanswered prayers, and the void left when God no longer feels near.

Written for those who have quietly slipped out of the pews and into a wilderness of doubt, grief, and inner searching, this is not a triumph story—but a survival story. A confession. A sacred wrestle. Through personal reflection and prophetic insight, the author unpacks what it means to climb without a safety net, to live without the scaffolding of religious performance, and to build a new compass in the absence of old crutches.

You haven't arrived. But you're still climbing. And that is holy.

NOW AVAILABLE:

www.amazon.com

It Was The God In

Success can be attributed to many things. Depending on the person who has obtained success would determine those to whom they attribute their success. Some give credit to their daily routine while others give credit to a mentor or some sort of system they followed. When I think about my success, the only person who I can give the credit to is God.

In this memoir, I share the successes and failures I have experienced throughout my life. From my individual experiences to my entrepreneurial journey, I share how God has walked with me every step of the way.

Come and see.. It Was The God In Me!!

NOW AVAILABLE:

www.amazon.com

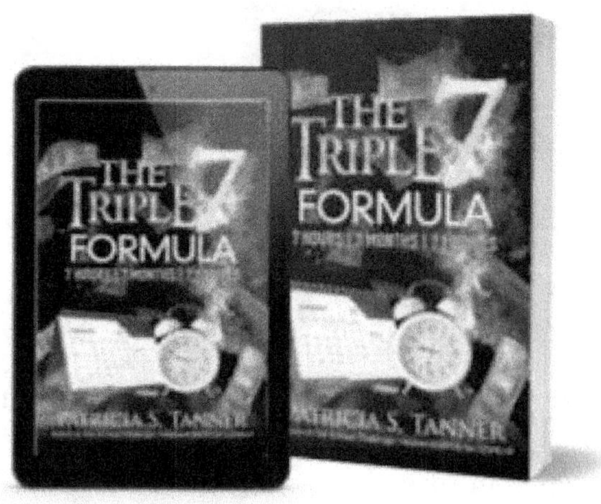

The Triple 7 Formula is designed for business owners who are looking forward to hitting the million-dollar mark in their business. If you own a business and seem to be running in financial circles, this book will get you on track to simultaneously gaining sound business structure and millions in your bank account.

It was through many conversations with business owners lacking financial gain that prompted Patricia to share her blueprint for millionaire status. Through this book, she demonstrates how to gain financial ground by developing strong teams, implementing systems, and setting stackable goals. If you are ready to gain a laser sharp focus, and implement these clear steps, you will position yourself for financial greatness. Your business will be sound, and you will see financial growth beyond your wildest dreams!!

NOW AVAILABLE:

www.amazon.com

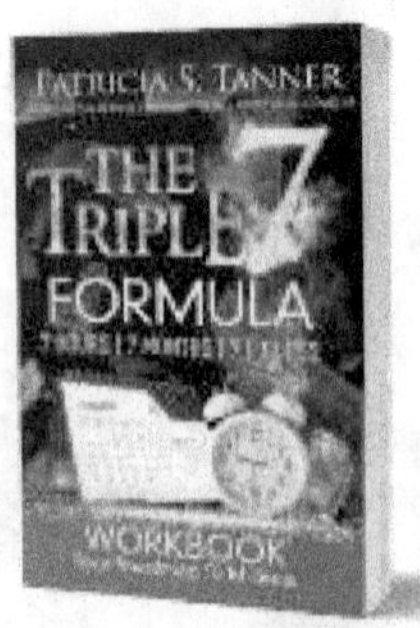

The Triple 7 Formula is specifically crafted for business owners aspiring to reach the million-dollar milestone. If you are a business owner feeling stuck in financial cycles, this book will set you on the path to building both a solid business structure and financial success.

This workbook is designed to complement the textbook of the same name. As you progress through its pages, you will be inspired to take decisive steps toward becoming a millionaire. From constructing your business framework to creating the millionaire's avatar, this process will expand your knowledge and mindset. Not only will you chart a course to financial success, but you will also identify your accountability circle and select a mentor to guide you toward greatness.

I cannot guarantee millionaire status unless you actively follow the steps to begin your journey. If you are searching for a get rich quick scheme, this workbook is not for you. I am looking for those ready to put in the effort—and since you are reading this, I believe that's you!

You have finally found it: Your roadmap to millions!

NOW AVAILABLE:
WWW.Amazon.com

Find Patricia on The Web:

www.PatriciaTanner.com

Follow Patricia on social media:

Facebook & Instagram: @PatriciaTannerInc